Rebecca Chapman is a barrister at Garden Court Chambers where she practises in all aspects of immigration, asylum and administrative law. She has particular expertise in cases involving vulnerable women and children, political asylum claims and cases brought on medical health grounds. Rebecca represents clients at all levels from the Tribunal to Grand Chamber of the European Court of Human Rights. She was appointed a Deputy Judge of the Upper Tribunal (Immigration & Asylum Chamber) in 2015.

Miranda Butler is a barrister at Garden Court Chambers. She has substantial experience across the spectrum of immigration, asylum, and public law. Her expertise includes claims relating to unlawful detention, prisoners' rights, trafficking, and community care. Having previously worked as a judicial assistant in the Supreme Court and European Court of Human Rights, Miranda currently teaches medical law at LSE alongside her practice.

A Practical Guide to Health and Medical Cases in Immigration Law

A Practical Guide to Health and Medical Cases in Immigration Law

Rebecca Chapman
Barrister

Miranda Butler
Barrister

Law Brief Publishing

© Rebecca Chapman & Miranda Butler

All rights reserved. No part of this publication may be reproduced, stored in a retrieval system, or transmitted, in any form or by any means, electronic, mechanical, photocopying, recording or otherwise, without the prior permission of the publisher.

Excerpts from judgments and statutes are Crown copyright. Any Crown Copyright material is reproduced with the permission of the Controller of OPSI and the Queen's Printer for Scotland. Some quotations may be licensed under the terms of the Open Government Licence (http://www.nationalarchives.gov.uk/doc/open-government-licence/version/3).

Cover image © iStockphoto.com/LaylaBird

The information in this book was believed to be correct at the time of writing. All content is for information purposes only and is not intended as legal advice. No liability is accepted by either the publisher or author for any errors or omissions (whether negligent or not) that it may contain. Professional advice should always be obtained before applying any information to particular circumstances.

Published 2021 by Law Brief Publishing, an imprint of Law Brief Publishing Ltd
30 The Parks
Minehead
Somerset
TA24 8BT

www.lawbriefpublishing.com

Paperback: 978-1-913715-51-9

This book is dedicated to my mother, Jenny Chapman Bryson. I would like to thank my partner Tolga and our son, Ben, for their support whilst writing this during the pandemic and various lockdowns.
- Rebecca

This book is dedicated to my partner, Nick Craigen. Many thanks to Amy Kerr for her invaluable assistance.
– Miranda

CONTENTS

Chapter One	Introduction	1
Chapter Two	Development of Article 3 Healthcare Cases	3
Chapter Three	The Principles Established by AM (Zimbabwe)	19
Chapter Four	Arguments in Support of an Article 3 Healthcare Claim	27
Chapter Five	Claims Based on the Risk of Suicide	35
Chapter Six	Article 8 Healthcare Claims	49
Chapter Seven	Healthcare Claims and the Refugee Convention	59
Chapter Eight	Fitness to Fly Challenges	61
Chapter Nine	Healthcare Claims Under EU Law	65
Chapter Ten	Convention on the Rights of Persons With Disabilities and Its Application in Domestic Courts	73

CHAPTER ONE

INTRODUCTION

We have been asked to write this book because health and medical cases have evolved into a discrete but important area within immigration law since the judgment in 1997 and the coming into force of the Human Rights Act 1998 on 2 October 2000. However, whilst human rights law makes provision for the protection against removal of migrants who have a serious illness, one of the challenges in arguing these cases has been the competing considerations between compassion for the extremely vulnerable against concerns about establishing a 'right to healthcare' for (usually non-settled) migrants, which has been termed 'health tourism'. This fails to take account of the fact that the majority of applicants have only become ill once they are already in the UK. In any event, since 6 April 2015, an NHS healthcare surcharge has been imposed for migrants seeking to enter the UK (currently £624 per person).

Another challenge is that a number of the test cases concern individuals facing deportation as a consequence of having committed following conviction for a criminal offence, often as a consequence of mental illness exacerbated by trauma experienced in the country of origin. Whilst the default position is that foreign national offenders will be deported, when there is evidence that the migrant in question suffers from a serious physical or mental illness and that appropriate treatment will not be available to them on return to their country of origin, their deportation may be contrary to Article 3 of the ECHR, which is an absolute prohibition on subjecting a person not only to torture but also to inhuman or degrading treatment or punishment. A further issue that has, from time to time, troubled the tribunals and courts since the judgments in *N*, is the morality of removing someone to a country where medical treatment is available, but they will be unable to afford to pay for it and therefore the likelihood is that their condition will deteriorate and they will die, but not necessarily imminently.

Happily, the reason that this book is timely is because the legal landscape in the UK has been changed significantly by *AM (Zimbabwe)* [2020] UKSC 17, judgment in which was handed down by the Supreme Court on 17 April 2020 and which has set out a new legal test for these cases. Whilst its implications have not yet been clarified by the lower courts and tribunals, we intend to provide the tools for practitioners to utilise in arguments in forthcoming cases, in order to contribute to a new body of jurisprudence on this issue in the future. Readers are also advised to look out for the forthcoming judgment of the Grand Chamber of the ECtHR in Savran v Denmark, which was heard on 24 June 2020 and will shed further light on consideration of article 3 cases involving mental health. See further Chapter 5, below.

Given that the focus of this guide is to be of practical assistance, we will set out a short history of the caselaw and then focus on how best to put forward a claim based on Articles 3 and 8 of ECHR and under the Refugee Convention, with reference to international caselaw and any other relevant Conventions. We have also included free standing chapters on cases involving a risk of suicide and fitness to fly challenges by way of judicial review. This book closes with two chapters on EU law and the CPRD which may be of more academic interest.

This book is being written during an international pandemic, which has forcefully brought to the world's attention the fact that diseases do not respect national boundaries. This book does not consider COVID-19 on its own because it should not be distinguished from other serious diseases in the immigration context.

This book covers the law on article 3 medical cases up to 18 February 2021.

CHAPTER TWO

DEVELOPMENT OF ARTICLE 3 HEALTHCARE CASES

Article 3 provides:

"No one shall be subjected to torture or to inhuman or degrading treatment or punishment."

This is an absolute right which makes no provision for exceptions and no derogation from it is permissible, even in the event of a public emergency.[1]

Scope of Article 3

Threshold of application

Notably, not all types of harsh treatment fall within the scope of article 3 as the Strasbourg Court has made clear in a number of cases that ill-treatment must attain a minimum level of severity. In *Ireland v. United Kingdom* (A/25) (1979-80) 2 E.H.R.R. 25, at [162], the Strasbourg Court held that the assessment of the minimum level of severity is relative: it depends on all the circumstances of the case, such as the duration of the treatment, its physical and mental effects and, in some cases, the sex, age and state of health of the victim.[2]

Type of ill-treatment to be established for the purpose of article 3

The Strasbourg Court accepted in *D v. United Kingdom* (App. No. 30240/96) (1997) 24 EHRR 423 that suffering caused by naturally

---

[1] See eg. *Chahal v UK* [1996] 23 EHRR 413.

[2] See also *Soering v. United Kingdom* (A/161) (1989) 11 E.H.R.R. 439.

occurring illness, be it physical or mental, may also fall under the protection of Article 3 where it is, or risks, being exacerbated by treatment for which the authorities are responsible: see further below.

Extraterritorial application

The Strasbourg Court has held that where '*substantial grounds have been shown for believing that the person concerned, if deported, faces a real risk of being subjected to treatment contrary to article 3*' the Convention requires that the victim not be removed to the country in question.[3] Conditions in the receiving country are to be assessed in light of the standards imposed by Article 3.[4]

Positive obligations

In general terms, Article 3 imposes a primarily negative obligation on States to refrain from inflicting serious harm on persons within their jurisdiction. However, as well as imposing negative obligations, Article 3 also imposes positive obligations upon Contracting States e.g. to refrain from certain actions; to take positive action to secure individuals their rights, and to protect them from prohibited treatment. Consequently, there is a positive dimension to the right that requires a State to take action to prevent inhuman or degrading treatment being inflicted by persons not acting on behalf the State. The Strasbourg Court confirmed in *L v. Lithuania* (App. No. 27527/03) (2008) 46 E.H.R.R. 22, at §46:

> "46. *The Court observes that the prohibition under Article 3 of the Convention is of an absolute nature, but that the kind of treatment qualified as inhuman and degrading will depend upon an examination of the facts of the specific case in order to establish whether the suffering caused was so severe as to fall within the ambit of this provision. Moreover, according to its established case-law, Article 3 entails*

---

[3] *Saadi v. Italy* [GC] (App. No. 37201/06) (2009) 49 E.H.R.R. 30, at [125]

[4] *Mamatkulov and Askarov v. Turkey* [GC] (App. Nos 46827/99 and 46951/99) (2005) 41 E.H.R.R. 25, at [67].

a positive obligation on the part of the State to protect the individual from acute ill-treatment, whether physical or mental, whatever its source. Thus if the source is a naturally occurring illness, the treatment for which could involve the responsibility of the State but is not forthcoming or is patently inadequate, an issue may arise under this provision (see, for example, D. v. the United Kingdom, 2 May 1997, §§ 51- 54, Reports of Judgments and Decisions 1997-III, and, mutatis mutandis, Pretty v. the United Kingdom, no. 2346/02, §§ 49-52, ECHR 2002- III)."

Unsurprisingly, the question that has arisen before both domestic courts and tribunals and the Strasbourg Court is the nature and extent of the applicable threshold *in circumstances where the harm results from naturally occurring illness* rather than the acts or omissions of State authorities.

D v UK[5] and establishment of the 'deathbed case'

D. was a national of St Kitts, who arrived in the UK in 1993 and sought leave to enter the United Kingdom for two weeks as a visitor. He was found to be in possession of a substantial quantity of cocaine, was refused leave to enter on the ground that his exclusion was conducive to the public good and given notice that he would be removed to St Kitts within a matter of days. D was then remanded in custody and prosecuted for the importation of controlled class A drugs. He pleaded guilty and was sentenced to six years' imprisonment. He was released on licence in 1996 and placed in immigration detention pending his removal to St Kitts. In August 1994, while serving his prison sentence, D suffered an attack of PCP and was diagnosed as HIV positive and as suffering from AIDS, having been infected some time before his arrival in the UK. Directions were made for D's removal to St Kitts in January 1996 whereupon his solicitors requested that the Secretary of State grant him leave to remain on compassionate grounds since his removal to St Kitts would entail the loss of the medical treatment which he was currently receiving, thereby

---

[5] [1997] 24 EHRR 423

shortening his life. This request was refused on 25 January 1996 by the Chief Immigration Officer on the basis that:

> "*While we are saddened to learn of Mr D[...]'s medical circumstances we do not accept, in line with Departmental Policy, that it is right generally or in the individual circumstances of this case, to allow an AIDS sufferer to remain here exceptionally when, as here, treatment in this country is carried out at public expense, under the National Health Service. Nor would it be fair to treat AIDS sufferers any differently from others suffering medical conditions...*"

D's application for judicial review of this decision was unsuccessful as was a renewed application to the Court of Appeal. D lodged an application with the European Court of Human Rights on 15 February 1996, arguing that his removal to St Kitts would be a violation of Articles 2, 3, 8 and 13 of ECHR. The Commission found in his favour in respect of Article 3. During an oral hearing before the Court the Appellant's argument at [40] was noted that:

> "*his removal to St Kitts would condemn him to spend his remaining days in pain and suffering in conditions of isolation, squalor and destitution. He had no close relatives or friends in St Kitts to attend to him as he approached death. He had no accommodation, no financial resources and no access to any means of social support.*"

At [53] the Court held:

> "*In view of these exceptional circumstances and bearing in mind the critical stage now reached in the applicant's fatal illness, the implementation of the decision to remove him to St Kitts would amount to inhuman treatment by the respondent State in violation of Article 3...Although it cannot be said that the conditions which would confront him in the receiving country are themselves a breach of the standards of Article 3 (art. 3), his removal would expose him to a real risk of dying under most distressing circumstances and would thus amount to inhuman treatment.*"

The Court found that the arguments in respect of Articles 2 and 8 did not raise any separate issues and in respect of Article 13, based on its previous judgments, the Court considered judicial review proceedings to be an effective remedy in relation to the complaints raised under Article 3 [70].

N v SSHD / UK[6] drawing the line at 'exceptional' cases

N was a national of Uganda, who entered the UK in 1998. She became seriously ill and was admitted to hospital, where she was diagnosed with AIDS. N made an asylum claim (not based on her health). Her appeal against this decision was dismissed but allowed by an Adjudicator on the basis that her case fell within the scope of the Asylum Directorate Instructions then in force, which provided that exceptional leave to remain in or enter the United Kingdom must be given:

> "... where there is credible medical evidence that return, due to the medical facilities in the country concerned, would reduce the applicant's life expectancy and subject him to acute physical and mental suffering, in circumstances where the UK [United Kingdom] can be regarded as having assumed responsibility for his care. ..."

The Secretary of State appealed to the Immigration Appeal Tribunal, who allowed the appeal. N's appeal to the Court of Appeal was dismissed, both judgments being predicated on the basis that there was not a complete absence of medical treatment in Uganda, Laws LJ holding at [40]:

> "... I would hold that the application of Article 3 where the complaint in essence is of want of resources in the applicant's home country (in contrast to what has been available in the country from which he is to be removed) is only justified where the humanitarian appeal of the case is so powerful that it could not in reason be resisted by the authorities of a civilised State. ...an Article 3 case of this kind must be based on

---

[6] [2005] UKHL 31; [2008] EHCR 453

facts which are not only exceptional, but extreme; extreme, that is, judged in the context of cases all or many of which (like this one) demand one's sympathy on pressing grounds ..."

On appeal to the House of Lords, N's appeal was again dismissed. The House of Lords, per Lord Nicholls, distinguished N's case from that of D on the basis that D was dying [13] & [15] refer]; see also Lord Hope at [36]. Lord Nicholls found the question that it is unacceptable to expel a person whose illness is irreversible and whose death is near but acceptable to expel a person whose illness is under control but whose death will occur once treatment ceases not to be capable of satisfactory humanitarian answers [13-14 refer]. Lord Hope held at [48] that the reason the Strasbourg Court held that exceptional circumstances were required in the *D* case was because of a departure from the principle at [54] in *D*. Lord Hope further held at [53]:

"[Any extension of the principles in D. v. the United Kingdom] would have the effect of affording all those in the [applicant's] condition a right of asylum in this country until such time as the standard of medical facilities available in their home countries for the treatment of HIV/Aids had reached that which is available in Europe. It would risk drawing into the United Kingdom large numbers of people already suffering from HIV in the hope that they too could remain here indefinitely so that they could take the benefit of the medical resources that are available in this country. This would result in a very great and no doubt unquantifiable commitment of resources which it is, to say the least, highly questionable the States Parties to the Convention would ever have agreed to."

On appeal to the Strasbourg Court, the Grand Chamber concluded:

"42. Aliens who are subject to expulsion cannot in principle claim any entitlement to remain in the territory of a Contracting State in order to continue to benefit from medical, social or other forms of assistance and services provided by the expelling State. The fact that the applicant's circumstances, including his life expectancy, would be

significantly reduced if he were to be removed from the Contracting State is not sufficient in itself to give rise to breach of Article 3. The decision to remove an alien who is suffering from a serious mental or physical illness to a country where the facilities for the treatment of that illness are inferior to those available in the Contracting State may raise an issue under Article 3, but only in a very exceptional case, where the humanitarian grounds against the removal are compelling. In the D. case the very exceptional circumstances were that the applicant was critically ill and appeared to be close to death, could not be guaranteed any nursing or medical care in his country of origin and had no family there willing or able to care for him or provide him with even a basic level of food, shelter or social support…

43. The Court does not exclude that there may be other very exceptional cases where the humanitarian considerations are equally compelling. However, it considers that it should maintain the high threshold set in D. v. the United Kingdom and applied in its subsequent case-law, which it regards as correct in principle, given that in such cases the alleged future harm would emanate not from the intentional acts or omissions of public authorities or non-State bodies, but instead from a naturally occurring illness and the lack of sufficient resources to deal with it in the receiving country."

Judges Tulkens, Bonello & Spielman issued a strong dissenting opinion, holding that the principle set out in *Pretty v UK* should:

"*equally apply where the harm stems from a naturally occurring illness and a lack of adequate resources to deal with it in the receiving country, if the minimum level of severity, in the given circumstances, is attained. Where a rigorous examination reveals substantial grounds for believing that expulsion will expose the person to a real risk of suffering inhuman or degrading treatment, removal would engage the removing State's responsibility under Article 3 of the Convention.*"

The dissenting Judges also criticised the majority in N for taking account of impermissible considerations (the burden on States obliged to provide free healthcare for aliens without the right to remain) as this was contrary to the absolute nature of Article 3.

In *Mwanje v Belgium*[7] six out of seven of the judges, including Judge Tulkens, issued a partially concurring separate opinion, in which they called for the case law in *N v. UK*, which they felt bound to follow to preserve legal certainty, to be reconsidered one day, as it set a very high threshold for Article 3 violation on the basis of compelling humanitarian grounds and required an extreme factual scenario where a person is at the final stage of a disease, near death, as was the case in *D v UK* in order to find a violation of Article 3. They considered that this was not compatible with the letter and spirit of Article 3 given the fundamental and absolute nature of this right and did not adequately respect the integrity and dignity of the person. Unfortunately, however, given the majority judgment in *N v UK* this was the view that prevailed for the following decade in relation to cases brought on the basis of ill-health.

MSS v Belgium and subsequent cases

In a separate line of authorities, however, beginning with *MSS v Belgium & Greece*[8] which concerned an Afghan asylum seeker who had passed through Greece *en route* to Belgium, who then sought to return him to Greece, the European Court of Human Rights held:

> *"263. In the light of the above and in view of the obligations incumbent on the Greek authorities under the European Reception Directive…, the Court considers that the Greek authorities have not had due regard to the applicant's vulnerability as an asylum seeker and must be held responsible, because of their inaction, for the situation in which he has found himself for several months, living in the street, with no resources or access to sanitary facilities, and without any means of providing for his essential needs. The Court considers that the applicant has been the victim of humiliating treatment showing a lack of respect*

---

[7] (2013) 56 EHRR 1140

[8] (2011) 53 EHRR 2

for his dignity and that this situation has, without doubt, aroused in him feelings of fear, anguish or inferiority capable of inducing desperation. It considers that such living conditions, combined with the prolonged uncertainty in which he has remained and the total lack of any prospects of his situation improving, have attained the level of severity required to fall within the scope of Article 3 of the Convention."

This was followed by *Sufi & Elmi v UK*[9] which concerned Somali nationals who the UK proposed to deport to Somalia. The Strasbourg Court held:

"282. If the dire humanitarian conditions in Somalia were solely or even predominantly attributable to poverty or to the State's lack of resources to deal with a naturally occurring phenomenon, such as a drought, the test in N v the United Kingdom may well have been considered to be the appropriate one. However, it is clear that while drought has contributed to the humanitarian crisis, that crisis is predominantly due to the direct and indirect actions of the parties to the conflict. The reports indicate that all parties to the conflict have employed indiscriminate methods of warfare in densely populated urban areas with no regard to the safety of the civilian population... This fact alone has resulted in widespread displacement and the breakdown of social, political and economic infrastructures. Moreover, the situation has been greatly exacerbated by al-Shabaab's refusal to permit international aid agencies to operate in the areas under its control, despite the fact that between a third and a half of all Somalis are living in a situation of serious deprivation."

283. Consequently, the Court does not consider the approach adopted in N v the United Kingdom to be appropriate in the circumstances of the present case. Rather, it prefers the approach adopted in MSS v Belgium and Greece, which requires it to have regard to an applicant's ability to cater for his most basic needs, such as food, hygiene and shelter, his vulnerability to ill-treatment and the prospect of his situation

---

[9] (2012) 54 EHRR 9

improving within a reasonable time-frame (see MSS v Belgium and Greece, cited above, paragraph 254)."

In *SHH v UK*[10] however, in which a severely disabled Afghani claimed that he would face a real risk of ill-treatment if he were returned to Afghanistan, the Strasbourg court referred both to *MSS* and *Sufi & Elmi* (paras 76 and 77) but followed neither, holding that the correct approach was that set out in *N v UK* and that no sufficiently exceptional circumstances were shown [95].

In *Tarakhel v Switzerland*[11] the Afghan asylum-seeking applicants claimed that if they were returned to Italy, they would be liable to be subjected to inhuman and degrading treatment linked to the existence of "systemic deficiencies" in the reception arrangements for asylum-seekers there. The Grand Chamber held at [122] following *MSS v Belgium & Greece* that:

> *"were the applicants to be returned to Italy without the Swiss authorities having first obtained individual guarantees from the Italian authorities that the applicants would be taken charge of in a manner adapted to the age of the children and that the family would be kept together, there would be a violation of Article 3 of the Convention."*

In *GS(India)*[12] which concerned a number of linked cases mainly involving applicants suffering from end stage kidney failure, the Applicants argued that the *MSS* line of reasoning should be adopted in preference to that of *N v UK* but this was firmly rejected, Lord Justice Laws holding:

> *"62. This learning shows that there may be departures from the Article 3 paradigm other than of the kind vouchsafed in D v UK. These departures are variously justified. But such an approach is indicated*

---

[10] (2013) 57 EHRR 18

[11] [2014] ECHR 1185

[12] [2015] EWCA Civ 40

in D itself, at paragraph 49, and in N at paragraph 43... In my judgment it is clear that the departures from the Article 3 paradigm given in MSS and the other cases to which I have referred do not extend the reach of the departure allowed in D and discussed at paragraphs 42 – 45 of N v UK. The plight of an individual whose life expectancy may be severely shortened by his removal or deportation to his home State is a distinct state of affairs whose treatment under the Convention is not qualified by the court's approach, for example, to the reception conditions for asylum-seekers. The circumstances in which a departure from the Article 3 paradigm is justified are variable; the common factor is that there exist very pressing reasons to hold the impugned State responsible for the claimant's plight. But the fact that there are other exceptions unlike D or N does not touch cases – such as these – where the claimant's appeal is to the very considerations which D and N address.

63. Accordingly, in my judgment, the Strasbourg jurisprudence in cases such as MSS and Sufi & Elmi casts no significant light on the approach to be taken by this court to the binding authority of N v Secretary of State in the House of Lords ... "

Applications were made to the European Court of Human Rights which were ultimately not determined due to the judgment in *Paposhvili v Belgium*[13] as a consequence of which the Secretary of State agreed to reconsider the cases.

Paposhvili v Belgium App. No 41738/10, 13.12.16

This landmark judgment concerned a Georgian national who was facing deportation due to criminal activity in Belgium but suffered from leukaemia and recurrent tuberculosis which had caused lung disease. He claimed that he would be unable to access adequate medical treatment in Georgia and was therefore at risk of ill-treatment in violation of Article 3 and accelerated death in breach of Article 2 if he were expelled there. His application to the Fifth Section was dismissed but his case was referred

---

[13] [2017] Imm AR 867

to the Grand Chamber and the applicant died pending those proceedings, which were continued by his family. The Grand Chamber held at [181]-[183]:

> "181. The Court concludes from this recapitulation of the case-law that the application of Article 3 of the Convention only in cases where the person facing expulsion is close to death, which has been its practice since the judgment in N. v. the United Kingdom, has deprived aliens who are seriously ill, but whose condition is less critical, of the benefit of that provision. As a corollary to this, the case-law subsequent to N. v. the United Kingdom has not provided more detailed guidance regarding the "very exceptional cases" referred to in N. v. the United Kingdom, other than the case contemplated in D. v. the United Kingdom.
>
> 182. In the light of the foregoing, and reiterating that it is essential that the Convention is interpreted and applied in a manner which renders its rights practical and effective and not theoretical and illusory (see Airey v. Ireland, 9 October 1979, § 26, Series A no. 32; Mamatkulov and Askarov v. Turkey [GC], nos. 46827/99 and 46951/99, § 121, ECHR 2005-I; and Hirsi Jamaa and Others v. Italy [GC], no. 27765/09, § 175, ECHR 2012), the Court is of the view that the approach adopted hitherto should be clarified.
>
> 183. The Court considers that the "other very exceptional cases" within the meaning of the judgment in N. v. the United Kingdom (§ 43) which may raise an issue under Article 3 should be understood to refer to situations involving the removal of a seriously ill person in which substantial grounds have been shown for believing that he or she, although not at imminent risk of dying, would face a real risk, on account of the absence of appropriate treatment in the receiving country or the lack of access to such treatment, of being exposed to a serious, rapid and irreversible decline in his or her state of health resulting in intense suffering or to a significant reduction in life expectancy…

186. …it is for the Applicants to adduce evidence capable of demonstrating that there are substantial grounds for believing that, if the measure complained of were to be implemented, they would be exposed to a real risk of being subjected to treatment contrary to Article 3. In this connection, it should be observed that a certain degree of speculation is inherent in the preventative purpose of Article 3 and that it is not a matter of requiring persons concerned to provide clear proof of their claim that they would be exposed to proscribed treatment.

187. Where such evidence is adduced, it is for the authorities of the returning State, in the context of domestic procedures, to dispel any doubts raised by it (see Saadi, cited above, § 129, and F.G. v. Sweden, cited above, § 120). The risk alleged must be subjected to close scrutiny (see Saadi, cited above, § 128; Sufi and Elmi v. the United Kingdom, nos. 8319/07 and 11449/07, § 214, 28 June 2011; Hirsi Jamaa and Others, cited above, § 116; and Tarakhel, cited above, § 104) in the course of which the authorities in the returning State must consider the foreseeable consequences of removal for the individual concerned in the receiving State, in the light of the general situation there and the individual's personal circumstances (see Vilvarajah and Others, cited above, § 108; El-Masri, cited above, § 213; and Tarakhel, cited above, § 105). The assessment of the risk as defined above (see paragraphs 183-84) must therefore take into consideration general sources such as reports of the World Health Organisation or of reputable non-governmental organisations and the medical certificates concerning the person in question.

188. As the Court has observed above (see paragraph 173), what is in issue here is the negative obligation not to expose persons to a risk of ill-treatment proscribed by Article 3. It follows that the impact of removal on the person concerned must be assessed by comparing his or her state of health prior to removal and how it would evolve after transfer to the receiving State.

189. As regards the factors to be taken into consideration, the authorities in the returning State must verify on a case-by-case basis whether the care generally available in the receiving State is sufficient and appropriate in practice for the treatment of the applicant's illness so as to prevent him or her being exposed to treatment contrary to Article 3 (see paragraph 183 above). The benchmark is not the level of care existing in the returning State; it is not a question of ascertaining whether the care in the receiving State would be equivalent or inferior to that provided by the health-care system in the returning State. Nor is it possible to derive from Article 3 a right to receive specific treatment in the receiving State which is not available to the rest of the population.

190. The authorities must also consider the extent to which the individual in question will actually have access to this care and these facilities in the receiving State. The Court observes in that regard that it has previously questioned the accessibility of care (see Aswat, cited above, § 55, and Tatar, cited above, §§ 47-49) and referred to the need to consider the cost of medication and treatment, the existence of a social and family network, and the distance to be travelled in order to have access to the required care (see Karagoz v. France (dec.), no. 47531/99, 15 November 2001; N. v. the United Kingdom, cited above, §§ 34-41, and the references cited therein; and E.O. v. Italy (dec.), cited above).

191. Where, after the relevant information has been examined, serious doubts persist regarding the impact of removal on the persons concerned – on account of the general situation in the receiving country and/or their individual situation – the returning State must obtain individual and sufficient assurances from the receiving State, as a precondition for removal, that appropriate treatment will be available and accessible to the persons concerned so that they do not find themselves in a situation contrary to Article 3 (on the subject of individual assurances, see Tarakhel, cited above, § 120)."

Clearly, whilst this judgment amended the test in *N v UK* the Upper Tribunal in *EA (Afghanistan)*[14] (Article 3 medical cases – Paposhvili not

---

[14] [2017] UKUT 445

applicable) and the Court of Appeal in *AM (Zimbabwe)*[15] declined to apply it on the basis that they remained bound by the judgment of the House of Lords in *N* and that remained the position until *AM (Zimbabwe)* reached the Supreme Court. Happily, the case of EA has subsequently been allowed on Article 3 grounds on appeal to the FtT and upheld by the UT.

---

[15] [2018] EWCA Civ 64

CHAPTER THREE

THE PRINCIPLES ESTABLISHED BY AM (ZIMBABWE)

AM (Zimbabwe) concerned a Zimbabwean national present in the UK since 2000, diagnosed as HIV positive in 2003 and facing deportation. Overturning the judgment in the Court of Appeal by Sales LJ (as he then was) the Supreme Court per Lord Wilson, applied the judgment in *Paposhvili* as to the effect of article 3 in deportation cases where it was claimed that an absence of appropriate medical treatment in the receiving country would result in a breach of the deportee's rights and in so doing, departed from the decision of the House of Lords in *N v. Secretary of State for the Home Department* [34]. The relevant test now is whether removal would give rise to a real risk of a serious, rapid and irreversible decline in the person's state of health resulting in intense suffering, or to a significant, meaning substantial [31] reduction in life expectancy. There is no longer a requirement that death be imminent in the event of removal. The Court held that:

> *"32. The threshold …is for the applicant to adduce evidence "capable of demonstrating that there are substantial grounds for believing" that article 3 would be violated…*
>
> *33. In the event that the applicant presents evidence to the standard addressed above, the returning state can seek to challenge or counter it in the manner helpfully outlined in the Paposhvili case at paras 187-191."*

Procedural requirements

The Supreme Court held at [32]:

> *"The Grand Chamber's pronouncements in the Paposhvili case about the procedural requirements of article 3, summarised in para 23 above, can on no view be regarded as mere clarification of what the court had previously said; and we may expect that, when it gives judgment in the Savran case, the Grand Chamber will shed light on the extent of the requirements. Yet observations on them may even now be made with reasonable confidence."*

The Supreme Court went on to hold at [23] applying *Paposhvili*:

(a) that courts should consider whether "*there are substantial grounds for believing*" that, if removed, they would be exposed to a real risk of subjection to treatment contrary to Article 3 (*Paposhvili* §186);

(b) where such evidence was adduced in support of an application under Article 3, it was for the returning state to "*dispel any doubts raised by it*"; to subject the alleged risk to close scrutiny; and to address reports of reputable organisations about treatment in the receiving state (*Paposhvili* §187);

(c) that the returning state had to "*verify on a case-by-case basis*" whether the care generally available in the receiving state was in practice sufficient to prevent the applicant's exposure to treatment contrary to Article 3; (*Paposhvili* §189)

(d) that the returning state also had to consider the accessibility of the treatment to the particular applicant, including by for applicants to adduce before the returning state evidence "*capable of demonstrating reference to its cost if any, to the existence of a family network and to its geographical location*" (*Paposhvili* §190); and

(e) that if, following examination of the relevant information, serious doubts continued to surround the impact of removal, the returning state had to obtain an individual assurance from the receiving state that appropriate treatment would be available and accessible to the applicant (*Paposhvili* §191).

Initial burden placed upon applicant

The first point to note is that the threshold is for an applicant to adduce evidence *'capable of demonstrating that there are substantial grounds for believing'* that article 3 would be violated. This is a **demanding threshold** for an applicant to cross, with the Supreme Court observing at [32] that: "*the requisite capacity of the evidence adduced by the applicant is to demonstrate "substantial" grounds for believing that it is a "very exceptional" case because of a "real" risk of subjection to "inhuman" treatment. All three parties accept that Sales LJ was correct, in para 16, to describe the threshold as an obligation on an applicant to raise a "prima facie case" of potential infringement of article 3. This means a case which, if not challenged or countered, would establish the infringement."*

The Supreme Court went on in the same paragraph to endorse the decision of the Upper Tribunal in *AXB v Secretary of State for the Home Department*:[16]

> "123. In a case where an individual asserts that his removal from the Returning State would violate his Article 3 ECHR rights because of the consequences to his health, the obligation on the authorities of a Returning State dealing with a health case is primarily one of examining the fears of an applicant as to what will occur following return and assessing the evidence. In order to fulfil its obligations, a Returning State must provide "appropriate procedures" to allow that examination and assessment to be carried out. In the UK, that is met in the first place by an examination of the case by the Secretary of State and then by an examination on appeal by the Tribunal and an assessment of the evidence before it."

As to the question of evidence, the Upper Tribunal held at [112]:

> "112. That acceptance however begs the question of what standard applies to that burden. Mr. Chirico did not suggest that we should lay

---

[16] [2019] UKUT 00397 (IAC)

down any hard and fast rule in this regard as he said that this is a matter of assessment in an individual case whether the evidence is sufficient. We accept that this may be so. However, we do not accept, as Mr. Chirico submitted, that what an appellant has to show must be to a lower threshold than an Article 3 risk. In our view, the words; that is to say the "ordinary" one of real risk or the higher one reserved for health cases. It is in that context that the Returning State has to provide evidence pointing the other way. As the Respondent points out, that can comprise (a) general evidence and (b) specific enquiries made by the Respondent of the authorities or other organisations in the Receiving State; and (c) the obtaining by the Respondent of specific assurances from the Receiving State relating to the Appellant.

Secretary of State to challenge or counter evidence adduced by applicant

Upon the applicant presenting evidence to the required standard, the Secretary of State can seek to challenge or counter it in the manner addressed at [23](b)-(e) of the judgment in *AM (Zimbabwe)*. Lord Wilson observed at [33]:

> "33. *The premise behind the guidance, surely reasonable, is that, while it is for the applicant to adduce evidence about his or her medical condition, current treatment (including the likely suitability of any other treatment) and the effect on him or her of inability to access it, the returning state is better able to collect evidence about the availability and accessibility of suitable treatment in the receiving state.*"

The Strasbourg Court in *Paposhvili* set out this duty at [189]:

> "189. *As regards the factors to be taken into consideration, the authorities in the returning State must verify on a case-by-case basis whether the care generally available in the receiving State is* **sufficient** *and* **appropriate** *in practice for the treatment of the applicant's illness so as to prevent him or her being exposed to treatment contrary to Article 3 (see paragraph 183 above). The benchmark is not the level of care existing in the returning State; it is not a question of ascertaining whether the*

care in the receiving State would be equivalent or inferior to that provided by the health-care system in the returning State. Nor is it possible to derive from Article 3 a right to receive specific treatment in the receiving State which is not available to the rest of the population."

Lord Wilson further clarified, with reference to the suggested obligation on the returning state to dispel "any" doubts raised by the applicant's evidence at [187] of *Paposhvili* that it is clear from [191] of that judgment that this means any "serious doubts".

If serious doubts remain the Secretary of State is to obtain individual assurances from receiving State

This is perhaps the most contentious aspect of the judgment in *Paposhvili*, given that in respect of the UK, previously assurances had really only been obtained in national security cases concerned with the risk of State inflicted torture or ill-treatment contrary to Article 3 of ECHR. In *Othman v United Kingdom*[17] an application concerning Abu Qatada's challenge to deportation from the UK, the Strasbourg Court developed a set of criteria to determine the reliability of diplomatic assurances that a returnee is not treated inhumanly in the receiving state ('diplomatic guarantees') at [187]–[189]:

> *"187. In any examination of whether an applicant faces a real risk of ill-treatment in the country to which he is to be removed, the Court will consider both the general human rights situation in that country and the particular characteristics of the applicant. In a case where assurances have been provided by the receiving State, those assurances constitute a further relevant factor which the Court will consider. However, assurances are not in themselves sufficient to ensure adequate protection against the risk of ill-treatment. There is an obligation to examine whether assurances provide, in their practical application, a sufficient guarantee that the applicant will be protected against the risk of ill-treatment. The weight to be given to assurances from the receiving*

---

[17] (App No. 8139/09) (2012) 55 E.H.R.R. 1

State depends, in each case, on the circumstances prevailing at the material time (see Saadi, cited above, § 148).

188. In assessing the practical application of assurances and determining what weight is to be given to them, the preliminary question is whether the general human rights situation in the receiving State excludes accepting any assurances whatsoever. However, it will only be in rare cases that the general situation in a country will mean that no weight at all can be given to assurances...

189. More usually, the Court will assess first, the quality of assurances given and, second, whether, in light of the receiving State's practices they can be relied upon. In doing so, the Court will have regard, inter alia, to the following factors:

(i) whether the terms of the assurances have been disclosed to the Court;

(ii) whether the assurances are specific or are general and vague;

(iii) who has given the assurances and whether that person can bind the receiving State;

(iv) if the assurances have been issued by the central government of the receiving State, whether local authorities can be expected to abide by them (Chahal, cited above, §§ 105-107) ...

(vi) whether they have been given by a Contracting State;

(vii) the length and strength of bilateral relations between the sending and receiving States, including the receiving State's record in abiding by similar assurances;

(viii) whether compliance with the assurances can be objectively verified through diplomatic or other monitoring mechanisms, including providing unfettered access to the applicant's lawyers ...

(xi) whether the reliability of the assurances has been examined by the domestic courts of the sending/Contracting State."

In *Tarakhel v. Switzerland*[18], which concerned the transfer to Italy of an asylum-seeking family pursuant to the Dublin III Regulation, the Court held that if there is a possibility that a significant number of asylum seekers may be left without suitable accommodation upon transfer, it was incumbent on the Swiss authorities to obtain assurances from their Italian counterparts that on their arrival in Italy the applicants would be received in facilities and in conditions adapted to the age of the children, and that the family would be kept together.

In *Secretary of State for the Home Department v Devani*[19] the Court of Appeal considered an appeal in which the applicant sought asylum having lost his challenge to his extradition to Kenya, holding as follows at [59]-[60] per Nicola Davies LJ:

"59. *The case law demonstrates:*

i) That the courts of England and Wales will, as a general rule, be reluctant to question the reliability of assurances provided by a requesting State in relation to prison conditions;

ii) An argument that a foreign State will not honour assurances represents a very serious allegation of bad faith and the evidence required to displace good faith must possess "special force" (Aswat above);

iii) There is no principle that assurances must eliminate all risk of inhuman treatment before they can be relied upon; the issue is whether no reasonable tribunal, properly instructed as to the relevant law, could have reached the same conclusion on the evidence (RB (Algeria) above);

iv) There is a fundamental presumption that a requesting State is acting in good faith and the burden of showing an abuse of process is on the person who asserts it, with the standard of proof being the balance of probabilities (Khan above).

---

[18] (App No. 29217/12) (2015) 60 E.H.R.R. 28; [2015] Imm. A.R. 282
[19] [2020] EWCA Civ 612; [2020] 1 WLR 2613

> "60. Underpinning the scrutiny which a court brings to assurances and any conclusions to be drawn from them is the principle of international comity and the public interest in upholding an effective system of extradition."

However, notably this judgment concerned a proposed extradition with concerns as to the prison conditions in Kenya, which is a very different factual matrix. Whilst no doubt the Secretary of State will seek to rely on the principles summarised above, we consider it is of limited relevance when the issue is the availability of sufficient and appropriate medical treatment, not least because what is sought is not an undertaking that a person will not be harmed but the particulars of any medical treatment available e.g. relevant medication, hospital and clinic facilities, cost and treatment in the community. It is also notable that, whilst Lord Wilson sought to throw limited light on the *'significant reduction in life expectancy'* limb, the Supreme Court did not engage in any detail with the alternate limb *viz 'serious, rapid and irreversible decline in health resulting in intense suffering'*. Consequently, this limb is likely to be subject to further litigation in the lower courts and tribunals.

CHAPTER FOUR

ARGUMENTS IN SUPPORT OF AN ARTICLE 3 HEALTHCARE CLAIM

Has the threshold been reached?

Firstly, it is necessary to identify if the applicant has an arguable case: has the applicant raised a *prima facie* case that there are substantial grounds for believing that removal would give rise to an Article 3 breach? Is the applicant seriously physically or mentally unwell and is there: "*a real risk, on account of the absence of appropriate treatment in the receiving country or the lack of access to such treatment, of being exposed to a serious, rapid and irreversible decline in his or her state of health resulting in intense suffering or to a significant reduction in life expectancy?*" If the issue is being raised as part of an asylum claim, then there is no requirement to make a separate application. However, if Article 3 is being raised purely on the basis of a medical or health case, then form FLR(HRO) should be completed and submitted. In exceptional circumstances, where the applicant is gravely ill and has only a matter of weeks to live, a letter with supporting medical evidence from his treating physician can be submitted in lieu of a formal application.

Notably, not only cases where there is an absence of appropriate treatment in the country of origin but given the inclusion of the phrase "*lack of access to such treatment*" it is at least arguable that an inability to afford to pay for treatment that is available meets the test. However, it will not be sufficient to simply assert that this is the case and it is likely to be necessary to show that the applicant not only lacks sufficient personal resources but also lacks a support network in the form of family and friends who could potentially assist in providing financial support. The Home Office frequently assert that this applies not only to extended family or friends in the country of origin, but also in the UK. Presenting Officers can be expected to question any supporting witnesses at appeal hearings as to their willingness and ability to provide financial support if the applicant is returned to their country of origin, so it is important if the case reaches an appeal to prepare witnesses and evidence accordingly.

Consideration should be given to whether an applicant suffering from a condition such as long Covid or who has underlying health conditions and is facing return to a country where there is no public health access to a vaccine against Coronavirus would reach the Article 3 threshold. Any application made on this basis would need to be very carefully evidenced.

Evidential requirements

Secondly, it is absolutely essential to provide clear evidence of the applicant's medical condition, including if possible, specialist evidence from a consultant as to diagnosis and prognosis, rather than simply documents such as the applicant's medical notes from the GP. It is also very likely to be necessary to obtain expert evidence as to the nature of any relevant medical treatment available in the proposed country of return, bearing in mind the standard of proof and the need to reach the threshold of showing a real risk of a breach of Article 3 or a *prima facie* case. This should include not only the availability of any medication required, but in a mental health case, the availability of any community-based treatment or support. Consideration will also need to be given to any support network in the form of family and friends, where in the country the applicant is likely to be living, both in terms of access to treatment and facilities and how the applicant will be financially supported. The Home Office guidance, *Medical claims under articles 3 and 8 of ECHR* version 8, recently updated on 19 October 2020 and addressed further below, provides at page 18 that the following evidence is required: medical condition; current treatment for their medical condition; the likely suitability of any alternate treatment for their medical condition and the effect that an inability to obtain effective treatment would have on their health.

At page 19 the Home Office guidance states that:

> "*There is no requirement to show that the claimant will receive equivalent treatment to that which they are receiving in the UK and that*

which is likely to be available and accessible in their country of return. Instead the relevant consideration is whether, despite the treatment that is available and accessible in the receiving country, the claimant is likely to suffer either a serious, rapid and irreversible decline in their state of health resulting in intense suffering or a substantial reduction in their life expectancy. Where treatment is available, you will need to consider if it is also accessible to the claimant in terms of costs and location (in relation to where they live) in the country of return, and what support they would have from family and friends. Whether medical treatment and care is accessible will involve consideration, in the round, of the cost of treatment from the state, from domestic and international nongovernmental organisations as well as assistance in obtaining treatment from state and private healthcare providers; support from family or friends in providing care and paying for treatment, and the claimant's own ability to afford treatment. In assessing if treatment is accessible you will also need to consider any physical obstacles that the claimant may need to overcome to obtain treatment. For example, they may live in a rural part of the country with limited transport options but have to travel to the only hospital that offers the relevant treatment in a city, hundreds of miles away."

Pages 32-34 of the guidance set out requirements for medical evidence, which places the onus squarely upon the claimants to provide "*acceptable, accurate and up-to-date medical evidence*" to support their application. Claimants must "*provide evidence about their current state of health and may also provide evidence as to the likely effect of return on their state of health.*"

There are also specific criteria for the form that the medical evidence must take i.e. that it needs to be "*printed on letter-headed paper showing: the address and contact details of the hospital or NHS trust, and the name and contact details of the consultant (note, private practitioners or medico-legal report writers may not be linked to a hospital or trust); an original document (hard or electronic version), not a photocopy or a faxed document; dated within 3 months of the date received by the Home Office (note, older evidence may: provide important context or information about the duration of an illness; confirm a person has a permanent and/or untreatable condition; be the most detailed medical report with later information providing an update on the situation); written and signed by a qualified health professional who must have seen the claimant with the medical condition in person (note, this may be via digital appointments) or is the clinician responsible for their care, accompanied with the medical practitioner's CV setting out their qualification experience and expertise (note, important medical evidence provided to the Home Office may be from clinician to clinician (for example, a memory clinic may send a report to the person's General Practitioner (GP) copying them in) or from clinician to patient and so may only include the person's name and job title."*

If the claimant is relying on expert evidence then the writer's expertise must be set out. The Home Office define *"a qualified health professional"* as a clinician who is primarily responsible for the claimant's day to day treatment, so long as that person is registered with the General Medical Council (GMC), or if not, reasons provided as to why not (e.g. retired). If the claimant is unable to meet these requirements then there is discretion to allow the claimant an opportunity to submit acceptable medical evidence within 28 days prior to a decision being made.

The guidance further provides that evidence of Post-Traumatic Stress Disorder will only be accepted when the medical report has been written by a consultant mental health specialist i.e. not a GP, unless the claimant is also able to provide an individual treatment plan developed with a mental health specialist.

There is also a prohibition on undue or indefinite delay in consideration of the claim, albeit the Home Office acknowledge that: *"it is important to consider if there are any exceptional circumstances which may mean the claimant is unable to notify the Home Office accordingly, for example but not limited to, due to; a particular disability, being detained under a section of the Mental Capacity Act; or if they lacked capacity to make such a decision."*

Home Office guidance 19 October 2020

Thirdly, check the Home Office guidance *"Medical claims under articles 3 and 8 of ECHR"* version 8, recently updated on 19 October 2020 and cite any relevant guidance specific to the case. It is also important to check for further updates to the guidance. The Home Office position at page 6 is that: *"leave is only granted on medical grounds in exceptional circumstances."* And at page 7:

> *"Policy intention: medical claims*
>
> *The policy intention in considering applications for leave to remain on medical grounds is to balance the needs of claimants who have serious medical conditions with the wider public interest by:*
>
> *• properly considering medical claims with sensitivity and granting leave outside the Immigration Rules in very exceptional cases, where there is strong medical evidence that removal would breach Article 3 or 8 of the ECHR*
>
> *• protecting finite NHS resources by removing those who have no right to remain here even where they have a medical condition, if that does not meet the very high threshold that applies in such cases*
>
> *• ensuring that access to health services does not act as an incentive for migrants to come to the UK illegally for medical treatment (health tourism.)"*

The reference here to exceptionality arises from *N* and the framing in *Paposhvili* at [183] to "other very exceptional cases." However, contrary to the policy intention above, there is no legal requirement or necessity to balance Article 3 with the wider or indeed any public interest.

As to the Secretary of State's response to the evidence, this is addressed at page 19 of the guidance and provides:

> *"you must investigate any serious doubts about whether they can be safely removed from the UK without breaching Article 3 on medical grounds. This must be done on a case by case basis, using evidence about the availability and accessibility of treatment in the receiving state to decide:*
>
> • *whether the care and treatment which is generally available in the receiving state is in practice sufficient to prevent a breach of Article 3, and*
>
> • *whether care and treatment is accessible, taking into consideration:*
>
> > o *cost*
> >
> > o *the existence of a family/support network, and*
> >
> > o *geographical location."*

The guidance provided as follows in respect of grants of leave at pages 35-36:

> *"Granting limited leave to remain*
>
> *If you decide an application meets the requirements for leave to remain based on a medical condition, you must grant DL.*
>
> *Length of grant*
>
> *You may grant DL usually up to a maximum of 30 months (two and a half years). It must not exceed life expectancy by more than 3 months, and you can grant leave in line with the length of treatment if it is appropriate."*

Given that the grant of leave is "usually" for only 30 months on a 10-year route to settlement and there is no indication as to whether or not public funds will be available, if there are arguments that the applicant is, for instance, a refugee then these will be definitely be worth making in order to obtain a grant of 5 years leave to remain. In any event, given that claimants seeking leave to remain in the United Kingdom on medical grounds are inherently likely to be vulnerable, it is worth putting forward arguments and expert evidence, if available, at the application stage as to the necessity to grant a longer period of leave, in line with the Home Office Discretionary Leave policy, so as to avoid the claimant having to undergo the cost and stress of making three further applications until s/he is entitled to ILR.

It is also worth checking whether the Home Office have produced a MEDCOI or CPIN report in respect of the country in issue and if they have, then it is very important to check the sources of the information relied upon and potentially challenge any sweeping assertions as the availability of eg medication and medical facilities with expert evidence.

Case management

Fourthly, if the application is refused and an appeal lodged, it is important to seek directions during case management hearings imposing strict deadlines for the Home Office to challenge or counter the evidence adduced on behalf of the applicant and, if necessary, to obtain assurances from the receiving State.

Cases based on mental health and the risk of suicide will be covered in Chapter 5.

It is also essential to prepare article 8 arguments in the alternative, in respect of which see Chapter 6. below.

CHAPTER FIVE

CLAIMS BASED ON THE RISK OF SUICIDE

Articles 2[20] and 3 ECHR place a positive obligation on public authorities to protect individuals from serious harm, including suicide where they are aware that a real risk of self-harm or suicide exists. This obligation applies in removal cases where there is a real risk that, as a result of the migrant's removal and / or deportation, they will attempt to commit suicide. Such cases are notoriously difficult to establish and domestic caselaw, principally *J v Secretary of State for the Home Department* [2005] EWCA Civ 629; [2005] Imm. A.R. 409, has set a high threshold for finding that removal would be in breach of Articles 2 or 3 ECHR due to suicide risk.

The rationale given for imposing such a high threshold in suicide cases has often involved a combination of the following:

    i.   The high threshold generally applicable in cases in which migrants seek to prevent removal on the grounds of ill-health;

    ii.   The inherent difficulties in establishing future risk of self-harm;

    iii.   Deference to assertions made by the Home Office about the adequacy of their mechanisms for preventing suicide prior to and during removal; and

---

[20] The case law discussed below exclusively focusses on Article 3 ECHR and it is therefore preferable to approach these cases under Article 3 ECHR. However, in a sufficiently clear case Article 2 ECHR may be engaged by a real and immediate threat to life: see e.g. *Rabone v Pennine Care NHS Foundation Trust* [2012] UKSC 2.

iv. A desire not to allow migrants to "*blackmail*" national authorities with threats of self-harm.

The authors' view is that such justifications do not justify imposing any higher threshold in suicide cases than that generally applicable in healthcare cases. A difference in approach has echoes of discredited medical practice which used to treat mental health issues as less 'serious' than physical health issues, and which failed to give mental health parity of esteem with physical health.[21] Suicide risk is capable of expert prognosis and where a real risk of suicide or self-harm exists this is sufficient to give rise to a breach of the person's right to life or to protection against inhuman and degrading treatment.

The domestic jurisprudence on suicide cases pre-dates *AM (Zimbabwe) v Secretary of State for the Home Department* [2020] UKSC 17, which has yet to be considered in the context of suicide. This chapter falls into two parts: firstly, examining the pre-*AM* caselaw and then considering how this may have changed since *AM*. We consider that the Supreme Court's lowering of the threshold for finding a violation of Article 3 ECHR should apply equally in cases involving suicide.

Caselaw pre-*AM*

In *J v Secretary of State for the Home Department* [2005] EWCA Civ 629; [2005] Imm. A.R. 409, the Court of Appeal considered the case of a Sri Lankan citizen who had been forced to work for Liberation Tigers of Tamil Eelam (the 'Tamil Tigers') and subsequently detained, interrogated and tortured by the Sri Lankan army. The Immigration Tribunal accepted J's account of his horrific treatment in Sri Lanka but found that he would not be at risk of further mistreatment on return. The psychiatric evidence established that J suffered from PTSD, severe depressive disorder and had attempted suicide, leading to inpatient treatment. His

---

[21] See *No health without mental health* (HM Government, 2011); s. 1 Health and Social Care Act 2012.

treating consultant psychiatrist opined that he would present with a very significant risk of suicide if forced to return to Sri Lanka.

Dyson LJ, giving the sole judgment, set out six principles which it considered were applicable in Article 3 suicide cases when determining whether there are "*strong grounds*" for concluding that there is a real risk of a breach of Article 3:

> v. An assessment was required of the severity of treatment which the applicant would suffer if removed;
>
> vi. A causal link must be shown between the act of removal and the inhuman treatment relied upon;
>
> vii. The Article 3 threshold is particularly high in 'foreign' cases, where the ill-treatment stems from a naturally occurring illness;
>
> viii. Nevertheless, an Article 3 ECHR claim can in principle succeed in a suicide case;
>
> ix. It is important whether the applicant's fear of ill-treatment is objectively well-founded. If a fear of ill-treatment is not well-founded, that would tend to weigh against finding a breach of Article 3;
>
> x. Whether the removing and / or receiving state have effective mechanisms to reduce the risk of suicide will be "*a question of considerable relevance*".[22]

In setting this high threshold, the Court applied *Ullah v Secretary of State for the Home Department* [2004] UKHL 26; [2004] 2 AC 323 to distinguish between 'foreign' and 'domestic' cases. 'Foreign' cases involve a claim that there would be a breach of an individual's human rights simply as a result of their removal to a third country. In such cases, it was

---

[22] Paragraphs 25 – 32.

necessary to show strong grounds for finding the existence of a real risk of torture of inhuman and degrading treatment.[23] Dyson LJ followed the Strasbourg Court's decision in *Bensaid v UK* (2001) 33 EHRR 10 and *D v UK* (1997) 24 EHRR 423 in concluding that there should be a high threshold set by Article 3 ECHR where the case does not concern the direct responsibility of the state.[24]

The Court of Appeal considered and approved *J* in *Tozlukaya v SSHD* [2006] EWCA Civ 379. The appellant and his wife were Turkish nationals who had entered Germany where their claim for asylum had been rejected. They had travelled to the UK with their child and against claimed asylum. The UK authorities asked Germany to 'take back' the appellant and his family under the Dublin Convention procedure. Germany had agreed to do so and the family's asylum claim had been refused and certified as a result. The appellant challenged the certification decision *inter alia* on the basis that his wife, W, would be at an increased risk of suicide if forcibly returned to Germany. The Court dismissed his appeal, holding that an increased risk of suicide was not itself a breach of Article 3 ECHR although it could amount to a breach in certain circumstances [67]. The application of Article 3 ECHR did not depend on an actual or potential breach of any Convention obligation by the receiving

---

[23] Quoting *Ullah* at [24]. There is an extensive discussion of 'domestic' suicide cases at [33] – [– 43], but such cases arise much more rarely in practice. In our experience, courts are very ready to accept that the mechanisms for averting suicides and self-harm while a person is within the UK are sufficient.

This stands in marked contrast to the latest available statistics on prison suicide which demonstrate that every five days a person in prison takes their life and for the seventh consecutive year, self-harm has remained at record levels: *Safety in custody quarterly bulletin,* dated 29 October 2020. Between April and June 2018 there were on average two suicide attempts every day: https://www.theguardian.com/uk-news/2018/oct/11/revealed-two-suicide-attempts-every-day-uk-deportation-detention-centres. No statistics on suicide in immigration detention are regularly published but in July 2020 the Home Office confirmed in response to a parliamentary question that self-harm in the immigration detention estate had risen to 474 cases requiring medical treatment in 2019 with 149 incidents merely up to 31 March 2020: https://questions-statements.parliament.uk/written-questions/detail/2020-07-07/70295.

[24] At [24].

state (following *Bensaid*) [57] – [– 58]. However, the effectiveness of the mechanisms in the receiving state to reduce the risk of suicide was a factor of "*considerable importance*" [59]. The Court accepted that the UK authorities would take reasonable measures to protect W against the risk of suicide prior to and during her removal from the UK. Appropriate measures would be taken by the German authorities following her return to that country, thus the appeal was dismissed.

One of the few successful suicide claims[25] is *Y and Z v SSHD* [2009] EWCA Civ 362; [2009] H.R.L.R. 22. This claim concerned a brother and sister who had been found by the Immigration Tribunal to have been tortured by the Sri Lankan security forces as suspected LTTE members or sympathisers, both had been raped in captivity, and both suffered from PTSD and depression. In addition to this tragedy, the siblings had lost various close family members as a result of state violence and mistreatment, while a further 50 family members in a tsunami which took place at the end of 2004. As in *J*, the Immigration Tribunal had found that there was no longer any real risk of mistreatment by the Sri Lankan authorities. Despite this, Sedley LJ (giving the sole judgment of the Court), held that "*a fear of renewed torture and sexual abuse may sometimes be just as real, and its potential consequences just as grave, when there is no longer a foundation for it*" [7]. He further pointed to the fact that a well-founded fear of persecution (which was the fifth important factor identified in *J*) would protect an applicant against removal under the Refugee Convention, leaving a claim under Article 3 academic. Such an approach "*leaves an unfilled space for cases like the present one where fear of ill-treatment on return, albeit held to be objectively without foundation, is subjectively not only real but overwhelming*" [14]. He reconciled this tension by explaining that "*One can accordingly add to the fifth principle in J that what may nevertheless be of equal importance is whether any genuine fear which the appellant may establish, albeit without an objective foundation, is such as to create*

---

[25] In fact the only successful reported judgments on this issue of which the authors are aware: see also *AJ (Liberia) v Home Secretary* [2006] EWCA Civ 1736 in which Hughes LJ, as he then was, remarked that no claim based on suicide risk had succeeded in any reported case.

a risk of suicide if there is an enforced return." [16]. Sedley LJ distinguished between this case and those where there are "*naturally-occurring illnesses*" as the appellants' condition was caused by severe mistreatment in Sri Lanka [50]. Upon return, they would be so "*subjectively terrified*" that they would be unable to access treatment and would face a "*subjective, immediate and acute*" risk of suicide [61; 63].

Y gives frustrated practitioners some indication of what may constitute a successful Article 3 claim based on suicide risk, namely:

    xi.   Severe subjective fear of return;

    xii.   Previous ill-treatment in the country of origin;

    xiii.   Where there will be no effective local mechanisms to avoid that risk of suicide, including where the applicant will be too subjectively terrified to access or benefit from treatment; and

    xiv.   The absence of other support mechanisms on return.

While these are useful indicators of what may make for a successful claim based on suicide risk, it would be a mistake to view the threshold for the engagement of Article 3 as requiring such extreme facts. Some immigration judges have been known to approach *Y and Z* on the basis that any factual scenario falling short of the appalling situation in which Y and Z found themselves must be unsustainable. In *YA (Somalia) v SSHD* (JR/5428/2019), handed down on 22 May 2020, the Upper Tribunal applied *Y* in concluding that Article 3 could be shown to be breached "*in an extreme case, where there is an independent basis for the fear giving rise to a genuine terror of return likely to prompt a successful suicide attempt*" [110]. On the basis of the authorities considered further below, we suggest that this sets the test for a breach of Article 3 too high and note that YA received permission to appeal to the Court of Appeal but the case was settled before a substantive hearing.

The most recent case of significance handed down before the Supreme Court's decision in *AM (Zimbabwe)* was *AXB (Article 3 health: obligations; suicide) Jamaica* [2019] UKUT 397. Much of the Tribunal's reasoning (including its analysis of *Paposhvili*) has now been superseded by the Supreme Court's decision as it only considers the Court of Appeal's decision in *AM (Zimbabwe)*. However, the Tribunal applies *RA (Sri Lanka) v Secretary of State for the Home Department* [2008] EWCA Civ 1210 and *Y* in concluding that the high threshold in Article 3 cases was that set out in *N v UK* [2008] ECHR 453 *"unless the risk involves the hostile actions of the Receiving State towards the individual"*. Therefore, notwithstanding any arguments about the effect of *AM (Zimbabwe)*, discussed below, practitioners should argue that a lower threshold applies in cases where the applicant has previously faced mistreatment in the country to which they face return.

Consideration of these issues is still ongoing in Strasbourg. The Fourth Section of the ECtHR applied the *Paposhvili* criteria in *Savran v Denmark* (No. 57467/15), which concerned the removal of a Turkish citizen with schizophrenia. The applicant had lived in Denmark since the age of six but had received a conviction of aggravated assault which led to the victim's death. Following this, in 2008 he was placed in the secure unit of a residential institution for the severely mentally ill for an indefinite period and received a deportation order. It was accepted by the applicant that his medical condition did not meet the threshold of *N* or *D* because it was stable due to a regime of medication, supervision, and psychological support. Significantly, the applicant's prescribed medication was available in Turkey and could be heavily subsidised or provided free of charge in appropriate cases. The Court accepted that, in addition to the medication which would be available in Turkey, a regime of supervision and support was essential. Applying *Paposhvili*, the ECtHR found in favour of the applicant, on the basis that Denmark had failed to ensure that a supervision scheme would be available and accessible to him particularly as his entire family resided in Denmark and would not be able to assist him in Turkey. This is a helpful decision to applicants as it emphasises the holistic nature of the approach to be taken when determining whether treatment is *"appropriate"* within the meaning of *Paposhvili*. The

Court accepted the relevance of factors such as cost, distance, barriers to access, the language in which care would be provided, and the existence of a social and family network (this being one of the *"important elements to take into account when assessing whether an individual has access to medical treatment in practice"*[26]).

However, on 27 January 2020, the Grand Chamber Panel accepted the Danish Government's request that the case be referred. Although the hearing occurred via video conference on 24 June 2020,[27] the judgment is yet to be delivered by the ECtHR. At the time of drafting a decision is awaited and is likely to be significant in either widening or narrowing the application of the *Paposhvili* test.

How to apply *AM* in suicide cases

At the time of writing, there has not been any significant judicial consideration of *AM (Zimbabwe)* in the context of claims based on the risk of suicide or self-harm. That is likely to change in the near future given the potential significance of the Supreme Court's decision and the frequency with which these claims arise in practice.

At [25] of *J* the Court rejected the submission on behalf of counsel for J that there should be a different test applicable in cases concerning a real risk of suicide or self-harm as opposed to claims based on physical health conditions. The Court explained at [42] that *"in our view, suicide cases should be approached in the manner that we have explained earlier. Cases concerning the risk of death resulting from the non-availability of treatment in the receiving state are not precisely analogous to those concerning the risk of suicide."* The Court expressly relied upon the line of jurisprudence including *Bensaid* and *D* which were overruled in *Paposhvili* and *AM (Zimbabwe)*.

---

[26] §62.

[27] Recording of the hearing is available at: https://www.echr.coe.int/Pages/home.aspx?p=hearings&w=5746715_24062020&language=lang&c=&py=2020

In *RA (Sri Lanka) v Secretary of State for the Home Department* [2008] EWCA Civ 1210 the Court of Appeal deprecated applying a different (and higher) threshold in mental health cases based on risk of suicide, holding at [49] that "*There has been some debate in our domestic case-law as to the extent to which cases of mental illness, in particular where it is said that removal will give rise to a risk or increased risk of suicide, are analogous to cases of physical illness for the purposes of the application of article 3 [...] Whilst there may be factual differences between the two types of case, the passage I have quoted from N v United Kingdom makes clear, as it seems to me, that the same principles are to be applied to them both*".

The Court of Appeal in *Wasif and another v Secretary of State for the Home Department [2016] EWCA Civ 82,* summarised the relevant authorities at [44] in relation to risk of suicide following removal and held that "*[i]t is clear from those authorities that such a claim will only succeed if there are 'exceptional circumstances' comparable in impact to those of the terminal patient in D v United Kingdom*". The high threshold in Article 3 suicide cases before *AM (Zimbabwe)* was therefore set at the same level as physical health cases.

There is therefore no sound reason to contend that the lowered threshold in *AM (Zimbabwe)* is not equally applicable in claims based on suicide or mental ill-health as in claims based on physical ill-health. It is notable that the Upper Tribunal in *KAM v SSHD* [2020] UKUT 269 (IAT) held at [52] that *AM (Zimbabwe)* had "*broaden[ed] the category of 'exceptional case' falling within Art 3 in medical / health cases*" generally. It should now be less difficult to succeed in an Article 3 claim based on the risk of suicide and the pre-*AM (Zimbabwe)* caselaw must be reconsidered in light of the Supreme Court's decision.

As discussed at greater length in chapter 3, the Supreme Court in *AM (Zimbabwe)* endorsed the ECtHR's test in *Paposhvili* at [183] that Article 3 would be breached where a "*seriously ill person*" could show "*substantial grounds*" for believing that they face a real risk "*on account of the absence of appropriate treatment in the receiving country or the lack of access to such treatment, of being exposed to a serious, rapid and irreversible decline in his or her state of health resulting in intense suffering or to a significant reduction in life expectancy*". We now consider each limb of this test in term in the context of suicide claims.

Seriously ill person. It is unlikely to be in dispute that any person who has been assessed as posing a risk of suicide as a result of mental health conditions would be seriously ill. NHS guidance defines severe mental illness as "*those people with psychological problems that are often so debilitating that their ability to engage in functional and occupational activities is severely impaired*".[28] Schizophrenia and bipolar disorder are treated by the NHS as severe mental illnesses. PTSD and associated conditions such as severe depressive disorders which impair day-to-day functioning and exacerbate risks of suicide or self-harm are plainly serious.

Substantial grounds. As we have seen, the caselaw before *AM (Zimbabwe)* referred to applicants establishing "*strong grounds*" in order to succeed in a claim under Article 3. That language was intended to reflect the very high threshold for finding a breach of Article 3 established in cases including *N, D, and Bensaid*. That threshold has arguably not changed, with the Supreme Court interpreting "*substantial grounds*" at [32] as representing a demanding threshold for applicants. The evidential standard therefore appears to remain high and practitioners in such cases must be seeking robust and detailed psychiatric evidence, preferably with input from the applicant's treating clinician, as well as expert country evidence about the conditions and availability of treatment in the receiving state.

Absence of appropriate treatment / lack of access to treatment. Arguments as to the absence and / or availability of appropriate treatment in physical or mental health cases are invariably a matter for expert evidence. The Home Office often relies on generic evidence to argue that drugs are available which will be capable of satisfactorily treating mental health problems, even where such problems are currently being treated with

---

[28] See, e.g. https://www.gov.uk/government/publications/severe-mental-illness-smi-physical-health-inequalities/severe-mental-illness-and-physical-health-inequalities-briefing

talking therapies and social support in addition to pharmaceutical intevention.

There may be a range of reasons why, in practice an applicant may be unable to access appropriate treatment. These include:

xv. Cost of treatment;

xvi. Low doctor-to-patient ratios making appropriately-qualified clinicians inaccessible;

xvii. Discriminatory, geographical and / or cultural barriers to treatment;

xviii. Availability of inappropriate treatment (including e.g. the availability of antidepressants where psychiatric evidence calls for therapeutic and pharmacological interventions).

Even where appropriate treatment is available to the applicant on return, it may be inaccessible or inappropriate for them depending on their circumstances. The very high rates of PTSD and related disorders amongst those making Article 3 claims based on suicide is highly relevant in this context; NICE guideline NG116 on PTSD[29] recognises that *"people with PTSD may be apprehensive, anxious, or ashamed. They may avoid treatment, believe that PTSD is untreatable, or have difficulty developing trust."*[30] Many individuals with PTSD and similar disorders are unable to benefit from available treatment until they feel subjectively safe, which usually requires an assurance that they will not be removed to a country where they consider themselves to be at risk. It is therefore important that representatives ask medical experts to opine on whether the recommended treatment would be effective in the applicant's circumstances if it were to be delivered in the country of origin following removal. If treatment requires subjective security which will not be available in a

---

[29] https://www.nice.org.uk/guidance/ng116/chapter/Recommendations#management-of-ptsd-in-children-young-people-and-adults

[30] §1.6.2

claimant's country of origin then there are good grounds to argue that this limb of the test endorsed in *AM (Zimbabwe)* is met.

Substantial decrease in life expectancy / intense suffering. A real risk of a successful suicide attempt is highly likely to bring with it a significant decrease in life expectancy. In *AM (Zimbabwe)* at [31] the Supreme Court interpreted "*significant*" as follows:

> "*[A] reduction in life expectancy to death in the near future is more likely to be significant than any other reduction. But even a reduction to death in the near future might be significant for one person but not for another. Take a person aged 74, with an expectancy of life normal for that age. Were that person's expectancy be reduced to, say, two years, the reduction might well – in this context – not be significant. But compare that person with one aged 24 with an expectancy of life normal for that age. Were his or her expectancy to be reduced to two years, the reduction might well be significant.*"

However, suicide risk linked to the act of removal is often likely to be immediate. While it will be a matter of the expert evidence in any given case, in the authors' experience most applicants who pose a significant risk of suicide or self-harm face particularly acute risks around the period of return to the country of origin. It is therefore likely that even elderly applicants who pose a real risk of suicide will face death in the near future and therefore should be able to show a significant reduction in life expectancy.

'Intense suffering' is unfortunately not considered by the Supreme Court at similar length. It is an open-textured term which should encompass both suffering due to psychiatric conditions and suffering which those conditions cause, including self-inflicted injury and suffering caused by an inability to function due to mental health problems, such as homelessness and destitution.

Substantial increase in the risk of suicide. The Court of Appeal in *J* rejected the argument that a substantial increase in the risk of suicide would lead to a breach of Article 3 ECHR. It had been recognised in *Soumaroho* *v SSHD* [2003] EWCA Civ 840 that "*[i]f it was arguable on the evidence that there was a real risk of a significantly increased risk that, if she were removed to France, the appellant would commit suicide, then in our view her claim based on Article 3 could not be certified as manifestly unfounded*", but this argument has not gained much traction since. Given *AM (Zimbabwe)*'s silence on how to approach suicide cases, this is an argument which merits further exploration. The Supreme Court's analysis of a decrease in life expectancy does suggest that if the risk of suicide in the near future became a more likely prospect then this should engage Article 3.

Procedural obligations. The Supreme Court has confirmed that, provided an applicant can raise a "*prima facie case*" of potential infringement under Article 3, if this is not challenged or countered then an infringement will be established [32]. This is not a new legal development; the Supreme Court notes that the Upper Tribunal in *AXB* reached the same conclusion at [112] and [123]. Nevertheless, it is useful to have confirmation from the highest judicial level that an applicant need only establish an unchallenged *prima facie* case in order to succeed in an Article 3 case. Of course in practice many claims based on suicide are challenged and countered (often successfully) by the Home Office's generic evidence, which paints a consistently optimistic picture about the standard of psychiatric healthcare available in other countries. This will therefore oblige practitioners to obtain more detailed expert evidence to counter the Home Office's response.

The procedural obligations discussed in *AM (Zimbabwe)* are therefore likely to be useful in urgent cases such as those involving injunctive relief to prevent removal. In such cases representatives can and should argue that un-countered allegations of an Article 3 breach should be sufficient to prevent removal, provided these have been properly evidenced.

CHAPTER SIX

ARTICLE 8 HEALTHCARE CLAIMS

Article 8 of the ECHR provides:

"1. Everyone has the right to respect for his private and family life, his home and his correspondence.

2. There shall be no interference by a public authority with the exercise of this right except such as is in accordance with the law and is necessary in a democratic society in the interests of national security, public safety or the economic wellbeing of the country, for the prevention of disorder or crime, for the protection of health or morals, or for the protection of the rights and freedoms of others."

The test for consideration of Article 8 in a medical case was set out in *Bensaid* (op cit), where the ECtHR held as follows:

"Not every act or measure which adversely affects moral or physical integrity will interfere with the right to respect to private life guaranteed by Article 8. However, the Court's case-law does not exclude that treatment which does not reach the severity of Article 3 treatment may nonetheless breach Article 8 in its private-life aspect where there are sufficiently adverse effects on physical and moral integrity (see Costello-Roberts v. the United Kingdom, judgment of 25 March 1993, Series A no. 247-C, pp. 60-61, § 36)."

Whilst on the facts of that case the Court found that removal of the applicant would not be disproportionate, the Court envisaged that there could be circumstances where it could be. In *MM (Zimbabwe)*[31] Moses LJ held as follows:

> "23. The only cases I can foresee where the absence of adequate medical treatment in the country to which a person is to be deported will be relevant to Article 8, is where it is an additional factor to be weighed in the balance, with other factors which by themselves engage Article 8. Suppose, in this case, the appellant had established firm family ties in this country, then the availability of continuing medical treatment here, coupled with his dependence on the family here for support, together establish 'private life' under Article 8. That conclusion would not involve a comparison between medical facilities here and those in Zimbabwe. Such a finding would not offend the principle expressed above that the United Kingdom is under no Convention obligation to provide medical treatment here when it is not available in the country to which the appellant is to be deported."

In *JA (Ivory Coast) & ES (Tanzania)*[32] the Court of Appeal emphasized that in contrasting claims made in health cases under Article 3 and Article 8 it is not simply a matter of the threshold of engagement being lower in bringing an Article 8 claim, because the outcome is subject to a test of proportionality unlike the absolute and unqualified nature of Article 3 in the protection it provides for, in respect of that which it excludes as a permissible consequence. Sedley LJ held at [16] – [17]:

> "*Here the prescribed purposes are, or include, the economic wellbeing of the country, which cannot afford to be the world's hospital, and the prior right of a settled population to the benefit of its inevitably finite health resources. Against these may legitimately be weighed both the moral duty to help others in need and the fact that the United Kingdom has until recently found it both morally compelling and economically*

---

[31] [2012] EWCA Civ 279

[32] [2009] EWCA Civ 1353

possible to extend such help to the appellants and others like them, alongside and not evidently to the detriment of the settled population.

There is no fixed relationship between Art. 3 and Art. 8. Typically a finding of a violation of the former may make a decision on the latter unnecessary; but the latter is not simply a more easily accessed version of the former. Each has to be approached and applied on its own terms..."

And at [17]:

"There is no fixed relationship between Art. 3 and Art. 8. Typically a finding of a violation of the former may make a decision on the latter unnecessary; but the latter is not simply a more easily accessed version of the former. Each has to be approached and applied on its own terms..."

It must be borne in mind that: "*article 8 is not article 3 with merely a lower threshold: it does not provide some sort of safety net where a medical case fails to satisfy the article 3 criteria.*"[33]

In *Akhalu (health claim: ECHR Article 8)*[34] the Home Office appealed against a decision by the First tier Tribunal to allow the appeal on Article 8 grounds. The appellant suffered from kidney failure and had had a transplant. It was accepted that she would be unable to afford the treatment she required in Nigeria and would die. Of note is the fact that "*the appellant has been considered to be someone in respect of whom the United Kingdom should be providing health care without charge, even after her period of leave to remain had expired: see Regulations 4(1)(iii) and (3) of the National Health Service (Charges to Overseas Visitors) Regulations 1989 (SI 1989/306) as amended.*" The Upper Tribunal upheld the decision of the FtT, holding:

---

[33] Per Hickinbottom LJ in SL (St Lucia) [2018] EWCA Civ 1894 at [27].

[34] [2013] UKUT 00400 (IAC)

> "47. Returning to the circumstances of this claimant we accept that it was open to the judge to find that this was one falling within what he had correctly recognised to be a very small number of cases that could succeed. In doing so he was not limiting his assessment to a comparison of medical treatment available here as compared with Nigeria. On the evidence before the judge, these were the factors that spoke in favour of the claimant's case:
>
> a. this was a claimant who had been lawfully present when she fell ill;
>
> b. she had been provided with medical treatment which she was recognised to be entitled to receive, without charge, from the NHS;
>
> c. it had been decided to treat her condition by providing a transplanted kidney which would require forever thereafter continued access to treatment of a different kind than she had needed before that, and that she live in a manner that could not be achieved should she be returned to Nigeria;
>
> d. that despite her illness and the demands of her treatment she had played an active part in community life and had thus established a level of private life that she could never hope to replicate in Nigeria;
>
> e. that the concession made before the judge meant that a major aspect of the reasoning leading to refusal of further leave had fallen away;
>
> f. that there was nothing in any way hypothetical or speculative about the inevitable difficult, early and unpleasant death that would follow return to Nigeria;
>
> g. contrary to the position as the respondent thought it was, the evidence established clearly that the claimant would meet that early death alone, and not with the support of her family."

However, much of the jurisprudence in respect of article 8 and medical cases precedes the coming into force of sections 117A-D of the Nationality, Immigration & Asylum Act ("NIAA") 2002, which set out the statutory public interest considerations that must now be taken into account both by the Home Office and by the Tribunals on appeal. A detailed analysis of these provisions is beyond the scope of this book but in essence, these provisions serve to limit the weight to be placed on a private life developed by the applicant when residing in the UK unlawfully or as an overstayer, unless section 117B(6) applies *viz* the person has a genuine and subsisting parental relationship with a qualifying child, and it would not be reasonable to expect the child to leave the UK. Where there is a decision to deport the applicant, then section 117C of the NIAA 2002 applies. There is no doubt that the introduction of these provisions has made it more difficult for an applicant to succeed in an article 8 case outside the Immigration Rules, however, the Courts have also made clear that ultimately, whilst a judge is not to conduct a free-range proportionality assessment, the decision has to be compliant with the principles of proportionality *cf. TZ (Pakistan)*.[35]

Children

In *R (SQ (Pakistan)) v Upper Tribunal (Immigration and Asylum Chamber)*,[36] the Court of Appeal noted that the question of whether or not the level of severity is reached to establish an Article 3 claim will depend on the circumstances of the case, recognising that there would be circumstances in which the threshold would be reached in relation to a child where it would not be reached in the case of an adult. In the context of an Article 8 medical claim, Maurice Kay LJ went on to observe that the decision in *ZH (Tanzania) v SSHD* [2011] UKSC 4: "*…demonstrates the central role of the best interests of a child in an Article 8 case*", adding at [26]: "*what this case demonstrates is that in some cases, particularly but not only in relation to children, Article 8 may raise issues separate from Article 3*". *SQ (Pakistan)* also makes plain that even in Article 8 cases involving children, the fact that the child is a "health tourist", if that is the case,

---

[35] [2018] EWCA Civ 1109 at [22]-[34]

[36] [2013] EWCA Civ 1251

and indeed the cost of the child's ongoing care to the state, will remain relevant to the proportionality analysis:

> "On the one hand, MQ can pray in aid his lawful entry and his status as a child with the protection of the ZH approach. On the other hand, he arrived with his serious medical conditions at an advanced stage and although not an unlawful entrant, it will be relevant to consider whether his arrival here was a manifestation of health tourism. If it was, that would fall to be weighed in the balance. After all, this country is under no international obligation always to act as the hospital of the world..." [27].

As to the Home Office guidance "*Medical claims under articles 3 and 8 of ECHR*" version 8, 19 October 2020, page 6 provides:

> "*The focus of Article 8 medical claims is on the quality of an individual's life, as set out in the Court of Appeal case of GS (India) & Ors v the SSHD [2015] EWCA Civ 40. Article 8 medical claims therefore form part of the balancing exercise which takes place when considering Article 8 claims although it should be noted that there must be a strong healthcare case before Article 8 is even engaged R (Razgar) v Secretary of State for the Home Department [2004] UKHL 27...*
>
> *This policy is designed to protect the National Health Service (NHS) and deter people from coming to the UK to seek free health care, so-called 'health tourism'. Disparities exist between healthcare systems around the world and it would place an intolerable and unrealistic burden on the finite resources available in the NHS if the UK were expected to provide free and unlimited healthcare to all those without a legal right to stay. That is why those who do not qualify to remain under any other provisions of the Immigration Rules are normally expected to leave the UK even where this would be difficult due to a serious physical or mental illness.*"

Clearly the Home Office position is that in the vast majority of cases, if an applicant does not succeed in respect of Article 3, they will not succeed in respect of Article 8 either, given the need to balance the applicant's medical condition against the cost to the NHS and the public interest. The exceptions to this may be where the applicant is a child or as per *MM (Zimbabwe)* where there are both family and private life elements to the Article 8 claim.

Organ transplants

These are specifically addressed at pages 25-27 of the Home Office guidance. In respect of pre-transplant cases:

> *"The fact that a claimant has been accepted in principle for an organ transplant is a factor you must take into account when considering the claim. In GS & Others, LJ Laws stated that: "Where there is a real possibility of a transplant in the near future, there may be a question whether ... removal from the UK before it was carried out would violate Article 3 on the specific footing that to deprive [a person] of such an imminent and transformative medical recourse amounts to inhumane treatment." However, as there can never be any guarantee of an organ becoming available, acceptance onto a transplant waiting list is unlikely to be a determinative factor that will lead to a grant of leave."*

However, whilst *GS (India)* was specifically concerned with ESKD, the test applied in that case in respect of Article 3 was that in *N* and thus the *AM (Zimbabwe)* test clearly impacts on the assessment of cases where a transplant is required. The Home Office position is that the Article 8 test viz *MM (Zimbabwe)* has not changed. The guidance continues to note that unless ordinarily resident in the UK, an applicant will fall into the category of group 2 patients eligible to receive a donated organ and thus:

> *"It is unlikely that a claimant currently waiting for a transplant will meet the required threshold unless their condition has deteriorated to such a point that they are in the critical stages of their illness. If a specific donor has been identified, for example a family member currently in the UK and the claimant has provided evidence that the transplant is likely to take place in the near future and could not take place in their country of origin; you must consider granting a period of leave to enable the transplant to take place. You must also consider whether*

55

> *evidence has been provided that indicates the procedure must take place in the UK. For example, if the donor is currently located in the country to where the claimant is to be removed, there must be reasons as to why the procedure cannot take place abroad."*

In respect of post-transplant cases, the fact that an applicant has received an organ transplant will be relevant to the overall Article 8 consideration *cf. Akhalu* (*op cit*). The rationale for distinguishing between pre- and post-transplant cases relates to the fact that in providing a donor organ, the state and the donor established an interest in the applicant remaining in the UK, in order to avoid rejection of the organ at a later date. The Tribunal also noted the low cost of anti-rejection medication compared with the cost of pre-transplant treatment and the possible consequences of removal. However, the Tribunal noted that the countervailing public interest in removal would outweigh an applicant's rights under Article 8 in '*all but a very few rare cases*'. The applicant in *Akhalu* had a highly developed private life in the UK which was considered to tip the balance.

The guidance provides at page 27:

> *"Accordingly, those who have received organ transplants will not normally be granted leave to remain in the UK solely to access ongoing medical treatment. However, in deciding whether to grant a period of leave and the duration of that leave you must consider the specific factors relevant to transplant cases, for example, the availability of anti-rejection medication, ability to follow lifestyle advice, access to medication and availability of healthcare and support abroad. In addition, you must take into account all other matters relevant to the Article 8 assessment – including, for example, whether the claimant is here lawfully or unlawfully, whether they are a health tourist and the extent of their family and private life in the UK."*

The guidance also provides that consideration should be given to granting a short period of leave in post-transplant cases, which are unlikely to meet the high threshold for Article 3 as applicants must produce evidence demonstrating that there are substantial grounds for believing that they would be exposed to a real risk of treatment contrary to Article 3. *"It is also likely that maintaining a transplant (through anti-rejection medication) will require less treatment over time and is significantly less expensive than, for example, dialysis. You must therefore consider whether the ability to access the necessary medication and support abroad will be easier to obtain as the claimant's condition improves. It may therefore be appropriate to grant a short period of leave, with a view to removal when the claimant's condition has stabilised."* The guidance further provides that transplant cases are not suitable for certification.

"No treatment" and "no serious and rapid decline" cases

As the Home Office guidance highlights at pages 19-20:

> *"Each of the limbs of the substantive test need to be satisfied. For example, the test is unlikely to be met in cases where the serious, rapid and irreversible decline in the claimant's health resulting in intense suffering or a significant reduction in life expectancy is not caused by the unavailability or inaccessibility of the required treatment on return. Similarly, the test is unlikely to be met in cases where even though the treatment the claimant needs is either unavailable or inaccessible on return, there is nevertheless no serious rapid and irreversible decline in the claimant's health resulting in intense suffering or a significant reduction in their life expectancy."*

There will be cases where the applicant's illness has become so advanced that there is no longer any medical treatment that would assist them or where the nature of the applicant's illness is such that their decline in health is slow rather than rapid. In these circumstances, if both limbs of the *AM (Zimbabwe)* test are not met, consideration should be given to focusing the claim around the applicant's Article 8 family and private life ties in the UK and potentially invoking the Home Office guidance in respect of Discretionary Leave at section 5 in respect of exceptional circumstances and non-standard grant periods : https://assets.publishing.service.gov.uk/government/uploads/system/uploads/attachment_data/file/658372/discretionary-leave-v7.0ext.pdf.

CHAPTER SEVEN

HEALTHCARE CLAIMS AND THE REFUGEE CONVENTION

If the applicant has expressed a subjective fear of persecution on return to their country of origin, then consideration should be given as to whether the applicant is a refugee within the meaning of the 1951 UN Convention on Refugees. Whether or not they are will depend on the reason for their fear and if it is because of their race, religion, nationality, membership of a particular social group or political opinion. The refugee claim may be entirely separate from the applicant's state of health and may be the reason they have come to the United Kingdom. Or it may be that the applicant's illness itself gives rise to membership of a particular social group *cf. DH (Particular Social Group: Mental Health) Afghanistan*[37] where the Upper Tribunal held that:

> *"Depending on the facts, a 'person living with disability or mental ill health' may qualify as a member of a Particular Social Group ("PSG") either as (i) sharing an innate characteristic or a common background that cannot be changed, or (ii) because they may be perceived as being different by the surrounding society and thus have a distinct identity in their country of origin... The assessment of whether a person living with disability or mental illness constitutes a member of a PSG is fact specific to be decided at the date of decision or hearing. The key issue is how an individual is viewed in the eyes of a potential persecutor making it possible that those suffering no, or a lesser degree of, disability or illness may also qualify as a PSG."*

Whilst the Home Office guidance at page 14 has a section in respect of "*Claims indicating Refugee Convention protection needs*" this is focused on the procedural aspect of making such a claim on the basis that the

---

[37] [2020] UKUT 223

applicant "*cannot access medical treatment in their home country for a reason which falls within the Refugee Convention, for example, being a member of a particular social group, because of their religious beliefs or political opinion or the evidence implies a fear of return for reasons other than those relating to their medical condition.*" In our view, consideration should always be given to whether the applicant is a member of a particular social group, albeit will be necessary to show that the applicant has a well-founded fear of persecution arising from membership of this group e.g. *LZ (homosexuals) Zimbabwe CG*.[38]

Please see further Chapter 9 in respect of EU law and in particular, claims made with regard to the Qualification Directive.

---

[38] [2011] UKUT 00487 (IAC)

CHAPTER EIGHT

FITNESS TO FLY CHALLENGES

Fitness to fly claims are some of the most challenging judicial review work that practitioners are likely to be involved in. Often last-minute, urgent and factually complex, these claims do not often lead to substantive decisions as successful challenges are generally settled before they can reach a substantive hearing and unsuccessful challenges sadly often result in unsafe and damaging removal of seriously ill individuals.

From the foregoing chapters, especially the discussion of *AM (Zimbabwe)*, it should be clear that there is a positive duty on the Home Office to conduct appropriate enquiries into the state of health of detainees and to investigate concerns if someone appears to be unfit to fly. A removal of a seriously unwell individual who is not fit to fly is likely to amount to a breach of Article 3 ECHR as a result of the damage to that person's health which may result. Similarly, seeking to remove a seriously unwell individual without proper assessment of their fitness to fly will likely be in breach of the Home Office's procedural obligations under Article 3 ECHR.

Home Office policy

The Home Office's *Arranging Removal*[39] guidance states that: "*You should assume that a detainee is fit to fly unless advised otherwise; however, if there is significant doubt as to the detainee's fitness to fly, you must request confirmation from the relevant healthcare provider.*" We would question whether "*significant doubt*" is consistent with the language of *AM (Zimbabwe)* that

---

[39] V. 2.0, 4 October 2018. Available at: https://assets.publishing.service.gov.uk/government/uploads/system/uploads/attachment_data/file/919645/arranging-removal-v2.0ext.pdf#page=9&zoom=100,92,804

potential returnees need only raise a "*prima facie case*" that their removal would be in breach of Article 3 ECHR.

Air travel guidance

International Air Travel Association (IATA) Medical Manual 9th Edition[40] contains a list of medical conditions and their suitability for travel by air. It also provides the following general guidance:

> "6.1.2: 'Medical clearance is required by the airline's medical department if the passenger:
>
> - *suffers from any disease which is believed to be actively contagious and communicable;*
>
> - *is likely to be a hazard or cause discomfort to other passengers because of the physical or behavioural condition,*
>
> - *is considered to be a potential hazard to the safety or punctuality of the flight including the possibility of diversion of the flight or an unscheduled landing;*
>
> - *is incapable of caring for himself and requires special assistance;*
>
> - *has a medical condition which may be adversely affected by the flight environment.*
>
> *Passengers not falling into the above categories normally do not need medical clearance, however, if in doubt, medical advice should be obtained.*"

The Civil Aviation *Assessing fitness to fly: guidance for health professionals* is a useful tool when determining whether a client is fit to fly. It confirms

---

[40] Available for download at https://www.iata.org/en/publications/medical-manual/

that the final decision whether to carry a passenger is for the airline.[41] It provides the following guidance regarding individuals with psychiatric conditions:[42]

> *"the key consideration in this area is identical to other medical conditions, i.e. will the condition interfere with the safe conduct of the flight or will the flight environment exacerbate the condition?*
>
> *[...] The main areas for concern are people whose behaviour may be unpredictable, aggressive, disorganised or disruptive. In the circumstances, air travel would be contra-indicated."*

Problems in practice

In most cases where fitness to fly is raised practitioners will meet with the same response from the Home Office: (i) our doctors have assessed the client and he is fit to travel; and (ii) the claimant will have adequate medical escorts in order to keep them safe during the flight.

The Home Office is under a duty to investigate and assess the fitness to fly of those it is seeking to remove, at least where they have raised a *prima facie* case that they are unfit to fly: *AM (Zimbabwe)* at [32]. The Home Office is also entitled to make a conscientious choice between competing pieces of medical opinion evidence: *ASK v SSHD* [2019] EWCA Civ 1239 at §220.[43] It may be hard to challenge such a choice by way of judicial review but the Home Office would nevertheless be bound by the traditional public law principles in choosing between medical evidence: taking into account all relevant factors, not taking into account irrelevant

---

[41] https://www.caa.co.uk/Passengers/Before-you-fly/Am-I-fit-to-fly/Guidance-for-health-professionals/Assessing-fitness-to-fly/

[42] https://www.caa.co.uk/Passengers/Before-you-fly/Am-I-fit-to-fly/Guidance-for-health-professionals/Psychiatric-conditions/

[43] This was in the context of the fitness of individuals with mental health illnesses to be detained and the Home Secretary making an assessment as to whether a particular serious mental illness could be satisfactorily managed in detention.

facts, acting fairly and rationally.[44] Pursuant to her duty of candour she would also be obliged to disclose all medical evidence relied on in such an assessment in the course of judicial review proceedings. In practice, Home Office medical assessments are often more superficial than assessments conducted by claimant's experts. It is helpful to scrutinise the quality of the assessment and, ideally, ask your own expert to respond to the Home Office evidence if time allows.

The provision of medical escorts during a flight is not a panacea. Effective medical treatment cannot be provided in an airplane in many cases. Forced removals will often be effected with heavy use of restraints which may be traumatising, especially for those who have been abused in custody. An individual who is not fit to fly may face serious and / or permanent physical or mental injury if they fly when they are not fit to do so. There is therefore good reason for practitioners to investigate and evidence the impact of removal on the physical and / or mental health of those being removed.

---

[44] See further *MN v SSHD* [2020] EWCA Civ 1746.

CHAPTER NINE

HEALTHCARE CLAIMS UNDER EU LAW

On 31 December 2020 at 11 pm ("**IP Completion Day**") the transition period ended and the European Communities Act 1972 ("**ECA**") ceased to have effect in the UK. The ECA was formally repealed on 31 January 2020 ("**Exit Day**") but was preserved during the transition period,[45] which has now ended. EU-derived domestic legislation as in force immediately before Exit Day continues to have effect in domestic law, subject to certain qualifications.[46] Direct EU legislation[47] which was operative immediately before IP Completion Day forms part of domestic law unless and until repealed. CJEU case law which was promulgated before Exit Day, will form part of retained EU case law where it is relevant to the interpretation of retained EU law, but is no longer binding on the Supreme Court or Court of Appeal.

This chapter sets out the protection for those with serious medical conditions under EU law. Readers are reminded that the Charter of Fundamental Rights and EU Directives[48] do not form part of domestic law after IP Completion Day.[49] However, while courts and tribunals will not be bound by EU law unless it is retained domestically, they may have regard to anything done on or after IP Completion Day by the CJEU, another

---

[45] European Union (Withdrawal) Act 2018 ("**EUWA 2018**"), ss. 1 – 1A.

[46] SsS. 1B, 2 EUWA 2018.

[47] This includes any EU Regulation, EU Decision, or EU tertiary legislation, provided it is not an exempt EU instrument under s. 20(1) and Schedule 6 EUQC 2018: s. 3 EUWA 2018.

[48] Legislation implementing Directives forms part of retained EU law.

[49] See s. 5 and Schedule 1 EUWA 2018.

EU entity or the EU so far as it is relevant to any matters before the court or tribunal.[50]

(i) Non-refoulement

The EU principle of non-refoulement is based in Art.19(2) CFR. Art.19(2) CFR directly corresponds to Art.3 ECHR[51] and, per Art.52(3) CFR, incorporates ECtHR caselaw regarding Art.3 ECHR. The principle of non-refoulement is a general principle of EU law (in the sense of Art.6 TEU).[52]

(ii) The EU Recast Qualification Directive (2011/95/EU)

The Qualification Directive broadly reflects the terms in Article 1A of the Geneva Convention. In *M'Bodj*[53] and *Abdida*,[54] the CJEU held that medical cases fall outside the scope of the Qualification Directive. The applicant in *M'Bodj* had been granted a residence permit in Belgium for medical reasons, on the basis that his removal to his country of origin would subject him to a real risk of inhuman or degrading treatment due to the lack of adequate treatment. Under Belgian law transposing the Qualification Directive, he had been granted neither refugee status nor subsidiary protection and had been denied income support. The CJEU ruled that a third country national with a deteriorating state of health, which was not the result of an intentional deprivation of health care, is

---

[50] s. 6 EUWA 2018.

[51] Explanations to Article 52 of the EU Charter on Fundamental Rights. Available at: https://fra.europa.eu/en/eu-charter/article/52-scope-and-interpretation-rights-and-principles

[52] Case C-465/07, *Meki Elgafaji, Noor Elgafaji v Staatssecretaris van Justitie* (17 Feburary 2009), para. 28

[53] C-542/13, *Mohamed M'Bodj v État belge* (18 December 2014)

[54] Case C-562/13, *Centre public d'action sociale d'Ottignies-Louvain- La-Neuve v Moussa Abdida* (18 December 2014)

not covered by Article 15 of the Qualification Directive[55] and therefore was not eligible for subsidiary protection. The CJEU held that since the Qualification Directive listed specific human activities as the *source* of persecution or serious harm, this form of 'serious harm' had to be the result of 'a form of conduct on behalf of a third party', so 'cannot therefore simply be the result of general shortcomings in the health system of the country of origin'.[56] This was supported by the Preamble, which in effect says that the Directive does not apply to those allowed to stay 'on a discretionary basis on compassionate or humanitarian grounds'. That the ECtHR interpreted Art.3 ECHR to mean that a person suffering from a serious illness could not be removed to a country with inadequate healthcare facilities, did not mean that they were necessarily entitled to subsidiary protection under the Qualification Directive. The CJEU made an exception for cases where the person concerned had been *intentionally* deprived of health care.

However, in the more recent case of *MP (Sri Lanka)*, the CJEU ruled that the Qualification Directive is to be interpreted in line with the CFR, itself to be interpreted in line with Art.3 ECHR.[57] The CJEU referred to *Paposhvili* in holding that a claimant who has been tortured in his country of origin but no longer faces a real risk of torture on return is eligible for subsidiary protection if he faces a real risk of being *intentionally* deprived of appropriate physical and psychological health care.[58]

---

[55] Which provides that subsidiary protection must be granted if the applicant is facing any one of the following three situations: (a) the 'death penalty or execution'; (b) 'torture or other inhuman or degrading treatment or punishment of an applicant in the country of origin'; or (c) 'serious and individual threat to a civilian's life or person by reason of indiscriminate violence in situations of international or internal armed conflict.

[56] C-542/13, *Mohamed M'Bodj v État belge* (18 December 2014), at paras. 35-37

[57] C-353/16, *MP v Secretary of State for the Home Department* (24 April 2018)

[58] At §at 51: "The risk of deterioration in the health of a third country national who is suffering from a serious illness, as a result of there being no appropriate treatment in his country of origin, is not sufficient, unless that third country national is

There is an argument that the Qualification Directive gives stronger protection to refugees than the Refugee Convention alone, namely that non-refoulement may have a wider meaning within the scope of EU law.[59] Although the wording of Article 14(4) Qualification Directive matches the non-refoulement rule in the Refugee Convention, the CFR, interpreted in line with ECtHR jurisprudence, sets a higher standard for non-refoulement. In *Chahal v United Kingdom* the ECtHR held that there was no 'room for balancing the risk of ill-treatment against the reasons for expulsion in determining whether a State's responsibility under Article 3…is engaged'.[60]

The Qualification Directive arguably offers limited protection in relation to serious ill health amounting to disability as compared to other protected characteristics. Disability is not expressly mentioned amongst the grounds of persecution that qualify for international protection, listed in Article 9 of the Directive. Second, there are several interpretative issues regarding the concept of a "particular social group" (PSG). The CJEU has laid down two conditions for a PSG.[61] First, members of the group must share an innate characteristic or a characteristic or belief that is so fundamental to identity or conscience that a person should not be forced to renounce it. Second, the group must have a distinct identity in the relevant country because it is perceived as different by the surrounding society. It has been argued that this poses a challenge for persons whose

---

intentionally deprived of health care, to warrant that person being granted subsidiary protection…"

[59] Boeles, P., 'Non-refoulement: is part of the EU's Qualification Directive invalid?' (EU Law Analysis, 14 January 2017). Available at: https://eulawanalysis.blogspot.com/2017/01/non-refoulement-is-part-of-eus.html?fbclid=IwAR1ThYi6ecdR1JBw1oqqRn9Wxu2l7oc0Hm6tmM-GAZfVjVAT_3i4Xiska1vU

[60] *Chahal v United Kingdom* App No.22414/93 (15 November 1996), at para. 81

[61] C-199/12, C-200/12 and C-201/12, *Minister voor Immigratie en Asiel v X, Y and Z* (7 November 2013)

disability is immutable but not visible.[62] Persons with disabilities are not always recognised as disabled by society. Third, the subjective fear requirement poses several difficulties to persons with mental or intellectual disabilities, who may lack the cognitive capacity to recognise dangerous situations. This leads some to argue that the individual conditions of persons with disabilities should be considered in order to determine whether there is a "well-founded fear".[63] However, the Directive does not facilitate such an approach: it does not invoke the principle of reasonable accommodation to assess the subjective element of the 'well-founded fear' of persecution and the objective risk of persecution.[64]

(iii) The Recast Reception Conditions Directive 2013/33/EU[65]

The Reception Conditions Directive requires Member States to take into account the special needs of vulnerable people who are seeking international protection. Per Article 21, persons with serious illnesses are vulnerable persons and have special reception needs. Article 11 provides that the health, including mental health, of applicants in detention who are vulnerable persons shall be of primary concern to national authorities. Member States have to ensure regular monitoring and adequate support for vulnerable persons, taking into account their particular situation and fragile health. However, Member States are accorded a wide margin of discretion.[66]

---

[62] Conte, C., 'What about Refugees with Disabilities? The interplay between EU Asylum Law and the UN Convention on the Rights of Persons with Disabilities' (2016) 18 *European Journal of Migration and Law* 327, 341

[63] *Ibid.*, 329

[64] *Ibid.*, 342

[65] Laying down standards for the reception of applicants for international protection (recast)

[66] *Ibid*, 348

(iv) The Return Directive 2008/115/EC[67]

The Return Directive requires detailed attention be paid to the particular situation of the vulnerable person (defined in Article 3(9) when adopting and implementing a return decision. Article 5 states that, when implementing the Directive, Member States shall take due account of (c) the state of health of the third-country national. Article

9(2) provides that Member States may postpone removal, taking into account the specific circumstances of the individual case, in particular (a) the third-country national's physical state or mental capacity. Article 14(1) lays down safeguards for this period of postponement, which include that (b) emergency health care and essential treatment of illness are provided and (d) special needs of vulnerable persons are taken into account. As to conditions of detention, Article 16(3) states that "particular attention shall be paid to the situation of vulnerable persons. Emergency health care and essential treatment of illness shall be provided".

Before *Abdida*, the matter of non-refoulement in relation to seriously ill migrants was treated as falling outside of EU law.[68] *Abdida* suggests that in some cases, those who do not qualify for subsidiary protection or refugee status (see discussion of *M'Bodj* above) can obtain protection under the Returns Directive. The case concerned a removal decision imposed by Belgium on a Nigerian national with AIDS, on the ground that the necessary care was available in his country of origin. While the Returns Directive does not require legal challenges to removal to have suspensive effect, the Court held that it was necessary to consider Article 19(2) CFR, interpreted in light of the ECtHR case law on Article 3 ECHR which

---

[67] Directive 2008/115/EC of the European Parliament and of the Council of 16 December 2008 on common standards and procedures in Member States for returning illegally staying third-country nationals

[68] Cornelisse, G. and Moraru, M., 'Judicial dialogue about the Return Directive: Which role for courts in an era of executive governance?' (Immigration and Asylum Law Policy, 1 September 2020). Available at: https://eumigrationlawblog.eu/judicial-dialogue-about-the-return-directive-which-role-for-courts-in-an-era-of-executive-governance/

bans removals on medical grounds in exceptional cases. The CJEU held that Articles 5 and 13 of the Return Directive, read in accordance with Articles 19(2) and 47 of the CFR and interpreted in light of ECtHR jurisprudence, require recognition of the suspensive effect of a remedy against a removal decision that would expose the applicant to a serious risk of a grave and irreversible deterioration of his health: Member States 'may not…proceed with…removal' where that 'would infringe the principle of non-refoulement'.

In *Abdida*, the CJEU committed itself to follow the case-law of the ECtHR regarding medical cases when interpreting the non-refoulement provision of the Returns Directive, there is a strong argument that it should follow that *Paposhvili* applies to the Returns Directive too.[69] If correct, this increases who can benefit from the EU law provisions regarding the suspensive effect of appeals and access to health care and social benefits.

What does this mean in practice?

The CJEU has recognised that there is protection for the seriously ill both in the context of asylum and immigration decisions. For now, the CJEU decisions referred to above will form part of retained EU law and may have effect domestically, but Courts are not bound to follow them.

Any new CJEU decision on these principles will merely have persuasive force in litigation now that the transition period has ended. Nevertheless, it may assist both judges and practitioners to be aware of the approach taken to these difficult cases elsewhere and work towards a harmonious approach with our neighbours.

---

[69] See Peroni, L., and Peers, S., 'Expulsion of seriously ill migrants: a new ECtHR ruling reshapes ECHR and EU law' (EU Law Analysis, 10 January 2017). Available at: http://eulawanalysis.blogspot.com/2017/01/expulsion-of-seriously-ill-migrants-new.html

CHAPTER TEN

CONVENTION ON THE RIGHTS OF PERSONS WITH DISABILITIES AND ITS APPLICATION IN DOMESTIC COURTS

The international law framework

The UN Convention on the Rights of Persons with Disabilities ('**CRPD**') was ratified by the UK in June 2009. However, it has never been incorporated into domestic law. The UK's dualist approach to international law means that it is not possible to advance a freestanding argument to the effect that an action or omission is not in compliance with the CRPD and thus unlawful.[70] Seeking to enforce unincorporated international law in domestic litigation is complex and practitioners interested in this topic are encouraged to refer to Shaheed Fatima QC's invaluable *Using international law in domestic courts*.[71] Generally, in order to rely unincorporated international law, it is necessary to rely on one of the following 'gateways':

- Showing that it is a part of customary international law ("**CIL**") and so part of English common law;[72]

---

[70] See e.g. *JH Rayner v Department of Trade and Industry* [1990] 2 AC 418, 476-477, 500; *Al-Saadoon* [2017] QB 1015, 269.

[71] October 2005, second edition due to be published in March 2021.

[72] See [78]-[91] of the Divisional Court's judgment in the *ISIS Beatles* case, *R (El Gizouli) v S of S for the Home Department* [2019] EWHC 60 (Admin).

- Showing that it is in any event already a part of English common law, perhaps as informed by international norms including under the ECHR;

- Showing that it is a breach of the ECHR (and, if applicable, other international conventions which may inform the interpretation of the ECHR) caught by s. 6 of the HRA 1998;

- Showing that it is engaged by a relevant statute, which:

    o must be interpreted compatibly with the ECHR (and, relatedly, other international conventions which may inform the interpretation of the ECHR) by virtue of s 3 of the HRA 1998 (see discussion above), and/or

    o is ambiguous and such ambiguity can be resolved by having recourse to the UK's international legal obligations, by application of the presumption that Parliament intends to act compatibly with those obligations;[73]

- Showing that it is part of domestic law by means of EU law (e.g. by means of the EU Charter of Fundamental Rights)[74];

- Showing, under ordinary domestic law principles, that there has been a self-direction as to the content of international law which is incorrect;[75] and/or

---

[73] *R v S of S for the Home Department, ex p Brind* [1991] UKHL 4

[74] Of course, this 'gateway' is of significantly less utility following the end of the transition period.

[75] *R v Secretary of State for the Home Department, ex p Launder* [1997] 1 WLR 839, 866-867; *R (Campaign for Nuclear Disarmament) v Prime Minister of the United Kingdom* [2003] 3 LRC 335, [36]; *R (Corner House)* [2009] 1 AC 756, [44] (Lord Bingham); *R (Davey) v Oxfordshire County Council* [2017] EWCA Civ 1308.

- Showing that there has been a failure to have regard to obligations under international law which are obviously material.[76]

Content of the CRPD

The CRPD creates disability-specific rights that are adapted specifically to address the challenges faced by persons with a disability. The Convention brought about a paradigm shift, emphasising the social model of disability[77] which recognises disabled persons as subjects and rights-holders.[78] The CRPD defines 'disability' broadly, to encompass long-term physical and intellectual disabilities and illnesses.[79]

The CRPD has the potential to enhance the international protection of asylum seekers.[80] However, refugees with disabilities are not directly addressed in the text of the CRPD: the CRPD does not, unlike the UNCRC,[81] specifically guarantee the rights of disabled refugees and asylum seekers. Nor are they directly addressed by the Committee on the Rights of Persons with Disabilities, in its General Comments or

---

[76] There may be some dispute over this; see, e.g., *R (Al Rawi) v Secretary of State for Foreign and Commonwealth Affairs* [2008] QB 289, [131]-[132], holding that it was for the decision-maker to decide whether the international legal obligation was a relevant consideration

[77] Article 1 recognises persons with disabilities to be 'those who have long-term … impairments which *in interaction with various barriers* may hinder their full and effective participation in society on an equal basis with others' [emphasis added]

[78] Crock, M., Ernst, C., McCallum, R., 'Where Disability and Displacement Intersect: Asylum Seekers and Refugees with Disabilities' (2013) 24(4) International Journal of Refugee Law 735, 737

[79] Article 1 protects persons with "long-term physical, mental, intellectual or sensory impairments."

[80] Conte (n12), 331

[81] Motz, S. 'The Persecution of Disabled Persons and the Duty of Reasonable Accommodation: An Analysis under International Refugee Law, the EU Recast Qualification Directive and the ECHR' in Bauloz et al (Eds.) *Seeking Asylum in the European Union* (Brill 2015), 145

examination of state reports and individual complaints.[82] Further, the relative novelty of the CRPD means that there has been little scholarly attention.[83] Therefore, there is, as yet, no cohesive analysis of its implications for refugee law.[84]

The rights and duties imposed by the CRPD include:

- A duty of reasonable accommodation, namely to make necessary and appropriate adjustments for disabled persons;[85]

- The right to equality and non-discrimination;[86]

- A duty to take all appropriate steps to ensure that reasonable accommodation is provided;[87]

- A right to liberty and security of the person, including freedom from arbitrary detention;[88]

- A right to be free from torture and cruel, inhuman or degrading treatment or punishment;[89]

- The right to health and to access health services;[90]

---

[82] Dimopoulos, A., 'An Enabling Interpretation of the 1951 Refugee Convention: Determination of Refugee Status in Light of the Convention on the Rights of Persons with Disabilities (CRPD)' in Burson and Cantor (Eds.) *Human Rights and the Refugee Definition: Comparative Legal Practice and Theory* (Brill 2016), 261

[83] Crock et al., 736

[84] Dimopoulos, 254

[85] Article 2.

[86] Article 5(1)-(2).

[87] Article 5(3).

[88] Article 14.

[89] Article 17.

[90] Article 25.

- The right to work, and to an adequate standard of living and social protection.[91]

However, this is only a duty of reasonableness and must not impose a disproportionate or undue burden on the state; given the prevailing financial constraints in many countries of origin this may mean little by way of actual support and protection for persons with disabilities.

It is unclear whether a breach of the duty of reasonable accommodation may amount to persecution.[92] As discussed elsewhere in this book, courts are reluctant to expand the duties on states to provide medical and social care for the seriously ill (and / or disabled) because of the potentially heavy financial burden this would place on the state. There are strong arguments against such an interpretation, including the statement in the UNHCR Handbook that 'serious violations of human rights' constitute persecution within the meaning of the Refugee Convention. Therefore, a sufficiently significant failure to provide reasonable accommodation could potentially amount to a serious human rights violation and qualify as persecution within the meaning of the Refugee Convention. The anti-discrimination principles at the heart of CRPD are useful interpretative aids here as refugee jurisprudence has sometimes been unwilling to recognise discriminatory treatment as persecution. It is at least arguable that the CPRD could encourage courts to take a more generous approach.[93]

In some cases, decision makers have also relied on the situation in the *host* country, highlighting the positive impact of the more specialised services and more inclusionary treatment received there, which in turn indicated the seriousness of the harm suffered in the country of origin.[94] It

---

[91] Article 27.

[92] Motz, 149.

[93] See e.g. Conte, C., 'What about Refugees with Disabilities? The interplay between EU Asylum Law and the UN Convention on the Rights of Persons with Disabilities' (2016) 18 *European Journal of Migration and Law* 327, 336.

[94] *AC (Egypt)* [2011] NZIPT 800015; *Dena Hernandez v Canada (Citizenship and Immigration)* [2010] FC 179 (CanLII)

should be noted that this is not an approach which has been endorsed in European jurisprudence: see e.g. *Savran v Denmark* at §60.

Article 11 CRPD makes specific reference to the rights of persons with disabilities in situations of risk and humanitarian emergencies. Art.11 places a positive obligation on States Parties to take all necessary measures in accordance with their international law obligations to ensure the protection and safety of persons with disabilities in situations of risk, including situations of armed conflict, humanitarian emergencies and the occurrence of natural disasters. It is, however, unclear whether this duty applies only to situations of risk in the country of origin or whether it also applies to persons applying for protection abroad.

The right in Article 18 to liberty of movement and nationality encompasses the right to "utilise relevant processes, such as immigration proceedings, that may be needed to facilitate exercise of the right to liberty of movement". This goes further than the ICCPR (Articles 12 and 24)[95] by extending the right to a nationality to disabled adults on an equal basis with others and by providing for a right to obtain, possess and utilise documentation of their nationality or other documentation of identification, or to utilise relevant processes such as immigration proceedings, that may be needed to facilitate exercise of the right to liberty. On ratifying the CRPD, the UK government entered a broad reservation regarding Article 18.[96]

---

[95] *Ibid.*, 146

[96] https://treaties.un.org/pages/ViewDetails.aspx?src=TREATY&mtdsg_no=IV-15&chapter=4&clang=_en#EndDec "The United Kingdom reserves the right to apply such legislation, insofar as it relates to the entry into, stay in and departure from the United Kingdom of those who do not have the right under the law of the United Kingdom to enter and remain in the United Kingdom, as it may deem necessary from time to time."

The Committee on the Rights of Persons with Disability has been slow to deal with the issue of non-refoulement.[97] In *O.O.J. v Sweden*[98] the Committee held that the principle of non-refoulement can be induced from the CRPD, but the case was declared inadmissible.

NL v Sweden[99] was the first case on non-refoulement that the Committee examined on the merits. This case concerned the deportation of a woman with physical and mental ill-health to her country of origin (Iraq) where she claimed she could not receive the necessary health care. The Applicant submitted a communication to the Committee, claiming that, by deporting her to Iraq, Sweden would violate her rights under Articles 6 (women with disabilities), 10 (right to life), 12 (equal recognition before the law) and 15 (freedom from torture or cruel, inhuman or degrading treatment or punishment) of the CRPD. The Committee considered that since the author had proved, with medical certificates, that her condition was 'severe and life-threatening' without adequate treatment, the returning State had to assess whether she would be able to access that medical care if removed to Iraq, which it failed to do. The Committee therefore found a violation of Art.15. The Committee noted the jurisprudence of the ECtHR in *Paposhvili*, both regarding the threshold to be reached by persons who are not in imminent danger of death in order to prevent their removal and on the assessment to be undertaken by the state regarding the availability and accessibility of care. *NL* is a striking example of cases which could be argued in terms of socio-economic rights (such as the right to the enjoyment of health under Article 25) being

---

[97] See Courtoy, M., 'Non-refoulement and access to healthcare: a first positioning by the Committee on the Rights of Persons with Disabilities', *Cahiers de l'EDEM*, November 2020. Available at: https://uclouvain.be/fr/instituts-recherche/juri/cedie/actualites/committee-on-the-rights-of-persons-with-disabilities-28-august-2020-n-l-v-sweden-communication-no-60-2019.html#_ftn5

[98] CRPD/C/18/D/28/2015, decision of 18 August 2017.

[99] CRPD, 28.08.2020, Communication No. 60.2019.

recharacterized in terms of inhuman treatment (here Articles 10 and 15) in order to allay judicial reticence to make decisions in socio-economic matters.[100]

Application of the CPRD in the UK

As discussed above, the CRPD is not directly enforceable in UK courts.[101] UK courts have not shown a sustained, systematic interpretation of CRPD provisions.[102] In a study conducted by Lawson and Series, there were, before 1 June 2016, 75 reported cases referring to the CRPD.[103] In 27 of these cases, there was no explicit reference to a particular provision of the CRPD.[104] In many of the cases in which explicit reference *was* made, this was often superficial or unsupported by discussion (for instance, only appearing in a footnote).[105] one was a decision of the Immigration and Asylum Chamber of the Upper Tribunal.[106] There were four cases on extradition and asylum.[107] Article 18 (liberty of movement and nationality) was not mentioned in any case.[108]

---

[100] See McAdam, J., 'Climate Change Displacement and Law: Complementary Protection Standards' (Legal and Protection Policy Research Series, May 2011), 17. Available at: https://www.unhcr.org/4dff16e99.pdf

[101] *Britliff v Birmingham City Council* [2019] UKEAT/0291/18/BA

[102] Lawson, A. 'The UN Convention on the Rights of Persons with Disabilities in UK Courts' (November 2018), 1.

[103] Lawson, A., and Series, L., 'United Kingdom', in Waddington and Lawson (Eds.) *The UN Convention on the Rights of Persons with Disabilities in Practice* (OUP 2018), 417.

[104] *Ibid.*, 429.

[105] *Ibid.*, 431.

[106] *Ibid.*, 427

[107] *Ibid.*, 434

[108] *Ibid.*, 429

The ECtHR and CJEU have made limited use of the CRPD in expulsion cases concerning persons with disabilities or serious illnesses. The ECtHR rarely uses the CRPD to advance an ECHR point; cases are generally decided under the broader ECHR framework, without taking account of the special needs of persons with a disability.

The UNHCR revised Resettlement Handbook (2011) moved away from the medical model[109] and aligned UNHCR policies more closely with the CRPD.[110] Further, the Executive Committee of the UNHCR expressly takes into account the contents of the CRPD for supporting the needs of refugees with disabilities, for instance stating that it is necessary to guarantee appropriate and reasonable standards of accessibility and to protect women and children with disabilities.[111] However, most decision-makers have not expressly engaged with a disability-sensitive interpretation of persecution.

In the UK, decision-makers have refrained from relying on the CRPD in order to define persecution. The Immigration and Asylum Chamber of the Upper Tribunal has been asked once to rely on the CRPD, in *RS & Ors (Zimbabwe – AIDS) Zimbabwe CG*.[112] This was in the context of the Disability Discrimination Act 1995. The UT rejected that the CRPD gave rise to justiciable legal obligations on the part of the Secretary of State, relying on the fact that the UK has specifically entered a very broad reservation to the liberty of movement guaranteed under Art.18 of the CRPD.

---

[109] I.e. the idea that disability is to be judged primarily by reference the fact of a diagnosis and a 'problem' to be 'fixed', rather than seeing disability as at least party constructed by surrounding society.

[110] Crock et al. 737

[111] Conte, 334

[112] *RS & Ors (Zimbabwe – AIDS) Zimbabwe CG* [2010] UKUT 363 (IAC).

HEALTH AND MEDICAL CASES IN IMMIGRATION LAW

In Australia, the CRPD has had a limited impact on judgments.[113] Waddington notes a "handful" of cases concerning asylum seekers with a disability and whose asylum claim related to their disability and the way they would allegedly be treated if returned to their state of origin or another state, in which the Australian Refugee Review Tribunal simply noted whether the State had ratified the CRPD.[114] Motz observes that in the case law of the Australian RRT, the CRPD has only been referred to as relevant for setting out the country of origin's obligations (in cases where the country of origin has ratified the CRPD), rather than as a human rights law framework relevant to the interpretation of 'persecution'.[115]

Disability-based claims have been recognised in Canada. *X v Canada* found "disabled minor" to be a 'particular social group' (PSG). It was found that there was a well-founded fear of persecution: the claimant had advanced clear and convincing proof of the state's inability to protect him because of his special circumstances due to his disability. Similarly, *X (Re)* found "disabled" (and women) to be a PSG[116], and *X (Re)* found "intellectual disability" to be a PSG[117]. *Ampong v Canada* found that the decision-maker failed to adequately consider discrimination against disabled persons in Ghana.[118] The court held it possible that the claimant may belong to a PSG. However, these cases did not refer to the CRPD.

---

[113] Waddington, L., 'Australia' in Waddington and Lawson (Eds.) *The UN Convention on the Rights of Persons with Disabilities in Practice* (OUP 2018), 73

[114] *10008207* [2010] RRTA 1117 and *1203800* [2012] RRTA 850. Waddington also notes a High Court decision, *Plaintiff M70/2011 v Minister for Immigration and Citizenship, Plaintiff M106/2011 v Minister for Immigration and Citizenship* [2011] HCA 32, in which documentation submitted to the court noted that Malaysia had ratified the CRPD. This was referred to in paragraphs 28 and 131 of the judgment.

[115] Motz, 161

[116] *X (Re)*, 2014 CanLII 90950 (CA IRB)

[117] *X (Re)*, 2012 CanLII 100292 (CA IRB)

[118] *Ampong v Canada (Citizenship and Immigration)* 2010 FC 35

Contrastingly, in *AC (Egypt)*, the New Zealand Immigration and Protection Tribunal took a disability-sensitive approach to the interpretation of the refugee concept in Article 1A(2) of the Refugee Convention via the standards expressed in the CRPD.[119] This case concerned an Egyptian Albino with a visual impairment. He had been socially marginalised in Egypt and experienced discrimination, harassment and physical violence. He had unsuccessfully tried to obtain work in the public and private sectors and as a self-employed person and had been unable to reply on Egyptian legislation seeking to promote disabled persons' access to the labour market. The New Zealand Immigration & Protection Tribunal found the claimant to be a refugee. The Tribunal stressed that he had been denied the very core of the right to work, and they also relied on the cumulative effects of the violence, discrimination in education and employment and isolation he had experienced. Egypt's failures under the CRPD effectively amounted to cumulative denials of reasonable accommodation. This has been identified as the first case to expressly recognise the relevance of the CRPD to the interpretation of 'persecution' and the only judgment to expressly refer to the duty of reasonable accommodation and the CRPD.[120]

The CRPD has thus not gained much traction as an interpretative tool in domestic law but remains a potentially useful interpretative aide.

---

[119] *AC (Egypt)* [2011] NZIPT 800015

[120] Motz (n23)., 168

MORE BOOKS BY LAW BRIEF PUBLISHING

A selection of our other titles available now:-

'A Practical Guide to Solicitor and Client Costs – 2nd Edition' by Robin Dunne
'Constructive Dismissal – Practice Pointers and Principles' by Benjimin Burgher
'A Practical Guide to Religion and Belief Discrimination Claims in the Workplace' by Kashif Ali
'A Practical Guide to the Law of Medical Treatment Decisions' by Ben Troke
'Fundamental Dishonesty and QOCS in Personal Injury Proceedings: Law and Practice' by Jake Rowley
'A Practical Guide to the Law in Relation to School Exclusions' by Charlotte Hadfield & Alice de Coverley
'A Practical Guide to Divorce for the Silver Separators' by Karin Walker
'The Right to be Forgotten – The Law and Practical Issues' by Melissa Stock
'A Practical Guide to Planning Law and Rights of Way in National Parks, the Broads and AONBs' by James Maurici QC, James Neill et al
'A Practical Guide to Election Law' by Tom Tabori
'A Practical Guide to the Law in Relation to Surrogacy' by Andrew Powell
'A Practical Guide to Claims Arising from Fatal Accidents – 2nd Edition' by James Patience
'A Practical Guide to the Ownership of Employee Inventions – From Entitlement to Compensation' by James Tumbridge & Ashley Roughton
'A Practical Guide to Asbestos Claims' by Jonathan Owen & Gareth McAloon
'A Practical Guide to Stamp Duty Land Tax in England and Northern Ireland' by Suzanne O'Hara
'A Practical Guide to the Law of Farming Partnerships' by Philip Whitcomb

'Covid-19, Homeworking and the Law – The Essential Guide to Employment and GDPR Issues' by Forbes Solicitors

'Covid-19, Force Majeure and Frustration of Contracts – The Essential Guide' by Keith Markham

'Covid-19 and Criminal Law – The Essential Guide' by Ramya Nagesh

'Covid-19 and Family Law in England and Wales – The Essential Guide' by Safda Mahmood

'A Practical Guide to the Law of Unlawful Eviction and Harassment – 2nd Edition' by Stephanie Lovegrove

'Covid-19, Residential Property, Equity Release and Enfranchisement – The Essential Guide' by Paul Sams and Louise Uphill

'Covid-19, Brexit and the Law of Commercial Leases – The Essential Guide' by Mark Shelton

'A Practical Guide to Costs in Personal Injury Claims – 2nd Edition' by Matthew Hoe

'A Practical Guide to the General Data Protection Regulation (GDPR) – 2nd Edition' by Keith Markham

'Ellis on Credit Hire – Sixth Edition' by Aidan Ellis & Tim Kevan

'A Practical Guide to Working with Litigants in Person and McKenzie Friends in Family Cases' by Stuart Barlow

'Protecting Unregistered Brands: A Practical Guide to the Law of Passing Off by Lorna Brazell

'A Practical Guide to Secondary Liability and Joint Enterprise Post-Jogee' by Joanne Cecil & James Mehigan

'A Practical Guide to the Pre-Action RTA Claims Protocol for Personal Injury Lawyers' by Antonia Ford

'A Practical Guide to Neighbour Disputes and the Law' by Alexander Walsh

'A Practical Guide to Forfeiture of Leases' by Mark Shelton

'A Practical Guide to Coercive Control for Legal Practitioners and Victims' by Rachel Horman

'A Practical Guide to Rights Over Airspace and Subsoil' by Daniel Gatty
'Tackling Disclosure in the Criminal Courts – A Practitioner's Guide' by Narita Bahra QC & Don Ramble
'A Practical Guide to the Law of Driverless Cars – Second Edition' by Alex Glassbrook, Emma Northey & Scarlett Milligan
'A Practical Guide to TOLATA Claims' by Greg Williams
'Artificial Intelligence – The Practical Legal Issues' by John Buyers
'A Practical Guide to the Law of Prescription in Scotland' by Andrew Foyle
'A Practical Guide to the Construction and Rectification of Wills and Trust Instruments' by Edward Hewitt
'A Practical Guide to the Law of Bullying and Harassment in the Workplace' by Philip Hyland
'How to Be a Freelance Solicitor: A Practical Guide to the SRA-Regulated Freelance Solicitor Model' by Paul Bennett
'A Practical Guide to Prison Injury Claims' by Malcolm Johnson
'A Practical Guide to the Small Claims Track' by Dominic Bright
'A Practical Guide to Advising Clients at the Police Station' by Colin Stephen McKeown-Beaumont
'A Practical Guide to Antisocial Behaviour Injunctions' by Iain Wightwick
'Practical Mediation: A Guide for Mediators, Advocates, Advisers, Lawyers, and Students in Civil, Commercial, Business, Property, Workplace, and Employment Cases' by Jonathan Dingle with John Sephton
'The Mini-Pupillage Workbook' by David Boyle
'A Practical Guide to Crofting Law' by Brian Inkster
'A Practical Guide to Spousal Maintenance' by Liz Cowell
'A Practical Guide to the Law of Domain Names and Cybersquatting' by Andrew Clemson
'A Practical Guide to the Law of Gender Pay Gap Reporting' by Harini Iyengar

'A Practical Guide to the Rights of Grandparents in Children Proceedings' by Stuart Barlow
'NHS Whistleblowing and the Law' by Joseph England
'Employment Law and the Gig Economy' by Nigel Mackay & Annie Powell
'A Practical Guide to Noise Induced Hearing Loss (NIHL) Claims' by Andrew Mckie, Ian Skeate, Gareth McAloon
'An Introduction to Beauty Negligence Claims – A Practical Guide for the Personal Injury Practitioner' by Greg Almond
'Intercompany Agreements for Transfer Pricing Compliance' by Paul Sutton
'Zen and the Art of Mediation' by Martin Plowman
'A Practical Guide to the SRA Principles, Individual and Law Firm Codes of Conduct 2019 – What Every Law Firm Needs to Know' by Paul Bennett
'A Practical Guide to Adoption for Family Lawyers' by Graham Pegg
'A Practical Guide to Industrial Disease Claims' by Andrew Mckie & Ian Skeate
'A Practical Guide to Redundancy' by Philip Hyland
'A Practical Guide to Vicarious Liability' by Mariel Irvine
'A Practical Guide to Applications for Landlord's Consent and Variation of Leases' by Mark Shelton
'A Practical Guide to Relief from Sanctions Post-Mitchell and Denton' by Peter Causton
'A Practical Guide to Equity Release for Advisors' by Paul Sams
'A Practical Guide to the Law Relating to Food' by Ian Thomas
'A Practical Guide to Financial Services Claims' by Chris Hegarty
'The Law of Houses in Multiple Occupation: A Practical Guide to HMO Proceedings' by Julian Hunt
'A Practical Guide to Unlawful Eviction and Harassment' by Stephanie Lovegrove
'Occupiers, Highways and Defective Premises Claims: A Practical Guide Post-Jackson – 2nd Edition' by Andrew Mckie

'A Practical Guide to Financial Ombudsman Service Claims' by Adam Temple & Robert Scrivenor
'A Practical Guide to Advising Schools on Employment Law' by Jonathan Holden
'A Practical Guide to Running Housing Disrepair and Cavity Wall Claims: 2nd Edition' by Andrew Mckie & Ian Skeate
'A Practical Guide to Holiday Sickness Claims – 2nd Edition' by Andrew Mckie & Ian Skeate
'Arguments and Tactics for Personal Injury and Clinical Negligence Claims' by Dorian Williams
'A Practical Guide to Drone Law' by Rufus Ballaster, Andrew Firman, Eleanor Clot
'A Practical Guide to Compliance for Personal Injury Firms Working With Claims Management Companies' by Paul Bennett
'A Practical Guide to Dog Law for Owners and Others' by Andrea Pitt
'RTA Allegations of Fraud in a Post-Jackson Era: The Handbook – 2nd Edition' by Andrew Mckie
'RTA Personal Injury Claims: A Practical Guide Post-Jackson' by Andrew Mckie
'On Experts: CPR35 for Lawyers and Experts' by David Boyle
'An Introduction to Personal Injury Law' by David Boyle
'A Practical Guide to Subtle Brain Injury Claims' by Pankaj Madan

These books and more are available to order online direct from the publisher at www.lawbriefpublishing.com, where you can also read free sample chapters. For any queries, contact us on 0844 587 2383 or mail@lawbriefpublishing.com.

Our books are also usually in stock at www.amazon.co.uk with free next day delivery for Prime members, and at good legal bookshops such as Wildy & Sons.

We are regularly launching new books in our series of practical day-to-day practitioners' guides. Visit our website and join our free newsletter to be kept informed and to receive special offers, free chapters, etc.

You can also follow us on Twitter at www.twitter.com/lawbriefpub.

Printed in Great Britain
by Amazon